Security without Obscurity

Security without Obscurity
A Guide to Cryptographic Architectures

J. J. Stapleton

CRC Press
Taylor & Francis Group
Boca Raton London New York

CRC Press is an imprint of the
Taylor & Francis Group, an **informa** business

AN AUERBACH BOOK

Published in 2019 by CRC Press
Taylor & Francis Group
6000 Broken Sound Parkway NW, Suite 300
Boca Raton, FL 33487-2742

Printed in the United States of America on acid-free paper
10 9 8 7 6 5 4 3 2 1

International Standard Book Number-13: 978-0-8153-9641-3 (hardback)

Visit the Taylor & Francis Web site at
www.taylorandfrancis.com

and the CRC Press Web site at
www.crcpress.com

Contents

Preface

This is the third book in the Security without Obscurity series. The first installment was my first book done on my very own. Previously, I had written articles and chapters for other peoples' books but not my own. The second book came about because of my collaboration with Clay Epstein and our decision to write a book together, and inadvertently created the series. At that time, I had no particular plans for a third book. The genesis for this book had several origins.

First, during my career, many times I have had to ferret out the cryptographic details for products, applications, and networks. From a crypto perspective, understanding the journalistic questions: who, what, why, where, when, and how is a critical aspect of information security. Too often the information is difficult to ascertain; misinformation and disinformation are not helpful. For example, vendors or service providers might be reluctant to reveal details, developers might have unreliable data, or product specifications are obsolete.

Further, vendors and service providers undergo mergers and acquisitions. Knowledge is often lost when employees or contractors depart. Product lines might be decommissioned and no longer supported. Products might not be updated and run with aging software. Product documentation might be dated or contain mistakes. Marketing sometimes makes unsubstantiated claims that are difficult to verify.

Second, the ability to conduct a security assessment in a reluctant or adversarial situation requires a set of skills that can only be learned by experience. However, there are dependable processes that can provide consistent results. Over the years, things to do and things not to do are included in lessons learned. These same processes work just as well for enthusiastic conditions. This book has an entire chapter on performing risk assessments.

Third, I published the article Cryptographic Architectures: Missing in Action in the July 2017 *ISSA Journal*. The article was on the journal cover, and it was republished in the Best Articles of 2017 in the January 2018 *ISSA Journal*. However, there was so much that I could have discussed, but a six-page article can only provide a limited amount of information. I provided the article to my publisher, and he agreed the topic would make another good book.

On another note, the ISSA article and this book refer to simple applications or network diagrams as cartoons. I personally credit Don Provencher* a former colleague at Bank of America, coining the term "cartoon" when referring to simplistic diagrams. Don was extremely knowledgeable about network architectures and was able to educate even me. We all miss you, Don.

In the first book, I mentioned my long-term participation with X9 standards. My participation and chairing the X9F4 workgroup endures to this day. The X9F4 program of work continues to grow with new standards and technical reports. Meanwhile, I continue to have a day job, work on X9 standards, and write this book. All of this with the loving support from my wife, Linda, and everyone still likes her best.

---

* www.legacy.com/obituaries/timesunion-albany/obituary.aspx?pid=186270529

Author

J. J. Stapleton has been involved with cryptography, public key infrastructure (PKI), key management, and numerous other information security technologies since 1989 when he attended his first Accredited Standards Committee X9 workgroup meeting. He has continued his X9 membership across many employers and has been chair of the X9F4 cryptographic protocol and application security workgroup since 1998.

- Jeff began as a software engineer at Citi Information Resources in 1982 when he was still working on his bachelors of science in computer science from the University of Missouri–St. Louis (UMSL).
- Jeff continued his career as a developer at MasterCard in 1984, managed developers on card payments applications, and began working on his masters of science in computer science from the University of Missouri–Rolla (UMR, now renamed Missouri Science and Technology). He also began his long-term X9 affiliation.

Jeff was assigned the design and development of a key management service (KMS) for the MasterCard network Banknet. The KMS was literally 24 hour from going live in production when a strategic decision to replace the then current IBM Series/1 minicomputers with a to-be-determined platform delayed the KMS project. He was able to take advantage of the experience by writing his thesis: Network Key Management in a Large Distributed Network, J. J. Stapleton, 1992, a thesis presented to the faculty of the Graduate School of UMR approved by Daniel C. St. Clair, Chaman L. Sabharwal, and James Hahn.

He actively participated in the development of the X9 technical guideline TG-3 personal identification number (PIN) Security Compliance Guideline (renumbered as technical report TR-39). The guideline provides evaluation criteria based on industry standards (X9.8 and X9.24) that defined security requirements for handling PINs and associated cryptographic keys. TG-3 was adopted by many payment networks for a biennial security assessment for interoperability.

Another accomplishment was his involvement in the development of the Secure Electronic Transaction (SET) specification, a joint venture between Visa and MasterCard for online card payments. As part of the SET project, he also worked with Netscape in their development of the Secure Socket Layer Protocol.

- Jeff joined Security Dynamics (renamed Rivest-Shamir-Adleman (RSA) Security) in 1996 when his division at MasterCard was sold to Global Payment Systems. He became part of RSA Labs, continued his X9 standards affiliation, and became the X9F4 workgroup chair.
- Jeff continued chairing X9F4 when he joined the auditing firm KPMG in 1998. SET had continued to evolve, and he led the KMPG team in the world-wide security assessment of the SET brand certification authorities (CA) in Japan, the United States, and France.

He actively participated in the development of the American National Standard X9.79 PKI Policy and Practices, and was involved with the American Institute of Certified Public Accountants (AICPA) in the adoption of X9.79 which eventually became the Webtrust for CA auditing standard. He also helped build the CA auditing program at KPMG.

He also assisted a major financial institution establish their first PKI including their certificate policy and certificate practice statement (CPS).

- Jeff was one of the founders of Cryptographic Assurance Services (CAS) in 2008, offering TG-3 assessments and Qualified Security Assessor (QSA) evaluations as a Payment Card Industry (PCI) certified company. He continued as the X9F4 chair.

In addition to performing numerous TG-3 assessments and QSA evaluation, Jeff assisted a major security company establish their first PKI including their certificate policy and CPS, key generation ceremony procedures, and completing a Webtrust for CA audit and Webtrust for Extended Validation audit.

- Jeff joined Bank of America in 2010 and eventually CAS ceased doing business when its contracts were completed. Meanwhile, he continued as the X9F4 chair and published the first *Security without Obscurity* in 2014.
- Jeff joined Wells Fargo in 2015, continued as the X9F4 chair, and published the second book *Security without Obscurity* in 2016.

Jeff is the primary author of the *Security without Obscurity* book series:

- *Security without Obscurity: A Guide to PKI Operations, February 2016*
  www.crcpress.com/Security-without-Obscurity-A-Guide-to-PKI-Operations/
  Stapleton-Epstein/p/book/9781498707473

■ *Security without Obscurity: A Guide to Confidentiality, Integrity, and Authentication, May 2014*
www.crcpress.com/Security-without-Obscurity-A-Guide-to-Confidentiality-Authentication/Stapleton/p/book/9781466592148

Jeff is also a contributing author to several other books discussing cryptography.

■ *Law Firm Cybersecurity*, Bill Spernow, Daniel B Garrie, ABA Book Publishing, 2017, ISBN: 978-1-63425-700-8
https://shop.americanbar.org/ebus/store/productdetails.aspx?productid=269327118
■ Chapter 16: Cloud Cryptography, Jeff Stapleton, *Information Security Management Handbook*, 6th Edition, Volume 7, Richard O'Hanley, Auerbach Publications, 2013
■ Chapter 20: Elliptic Curve Cryptosystems, Jeff Stapleton, *Information Security Management Handbook*, 6th Edition, Volume 6, Harold F. Tipton, Auerbach Publications, 2012, ISBN 978-1-4398-9313-5
■ Chapter 23: Cryptographic Message Syntax (CMS), Jeff Stapleton, *Information Security Management Handbook*, 6th Edition, Volume 5, Harold F. Tipton, Auerbach Publications, 2011, ISBN 978-1-46650850-7
■ Chapter 17: Trusted Time Stamps, Jeff Stapleton, *Information Security Management Handbook*, 6th Edition, Volume 4, Harold F. Tipton, Auerbach Publications, 2010, ISBN 978-1-4398-1903-6
■ *PKI*, Thomas Austin, contributing authors – Santosh Chokhani, Roseann Day, Todd Glassey, Sven Hammar, Diana Kelley, Sathvik Krishnamurthy, Steve McIntosh, Samir Nanavati, Ruven Schwartz, Jeff Stapleton, A Wile Tech Brief, 2001, ISBN 0-471-35380-9
■ *Biometrics*, John D. Woodward Jr., Nicholas M. Orlans, Peter T. Higgins, contributing authors: Dr. Martin Libicki, Kapil Raina, Richard E. Smith, Jeff Stapleton, Dr. Valorie Valencia, McGraw-Hill/Osborne, 1999, ISBN 0-07-222227-1

Jeff has published several papers on cryptography.

■ Cryptographic Transitions, Jeff Stapleton, Ralph Poore, IEEE 1-4244-0359-6/06, 2006
■ Digital Signature Paradox, Jeff Stapleton, Paul Doyle, Steven Teppler Esquire, IEEE Workshop on Information Assurance and Security, United States Military Academy, West Point, NY, 2005
■ PKI Note: Smart Cards, Eric Longo, Jeff Stapleton, PKI Forum, 2002
■ PKI Note: CA Trust, Jeff Stapleton, PKI Forum, 2001
■ PKI Note: Biometrics, Jeff Stapleton, PKI Forum, 2001

- A Biometric Standard for Information Management and Security, Stephen M. Matyas Jr., Jeff Stapleton, *Computers & Security*, Elsevier Science, 2000

Jeff has written numerous articles in various information security journals.

- Best Articles of 2017, Cryptographic Architectures: Missing in Action, Jeff Stapleton, *ISSA Journal*, January 2018
- Cryptographic Architectures: Missing in Action, Jeff Stapleton, *ISSA Journal*, July 2017 was the journal cover article
- Gaining Confidence in the Cloud, Phillip Griffin, Jeff Stapleton, *ISSA Journal*, January 2016
- Mobile Security Banking and Payments Standard, Jeff Stapleton, *ISSA Journal*, June 2014
- Crypto in Crisis: Heartbleed, Jeff Stapleton, *ISSA Journal*, June 2014
- Cloud Services Compliance Data Standard, Jeff Stapleton, *ISSA Journal*, April 2014
- PKI Under Attack, Jeff Stapleton, *ISSA Journal*, March 2013
- Brief History of PKI, Jeff Stapleton, *ISSA Journal*, September 2012
- The Art of Exception, Jeff Stapleton, Ben Cobb, *ISSA Journal*, July 2011
- Tokenization and Other Methods of Security Cardholder, Ralph Poore, Jeff Stapleton *(ISC)² Information Security Journal*, 2010
- PAN Encryption: The next evolutionary step?, Jeff Stapleton, *ISSA Journal*, June 2009
- The PCI DSS: Friend or foe?, Jeff Stapleton, *ISSA Journal*, April 2009
- Cryptography as a Service, Jeff Stapleton, *ISSA Journal*, January 2009
- Digital Signatures Are Not Enough, Jeff Stapleton, Steven Teppler, *ISSA Journal*, January 2006 was the journal cover article.

Jeff has participated in the development of over three dozen X9 standards, half-a-dozen international ISO standards, and has been a U.S. expert to several ISO Technical Committees, 68 subcommittees, and workgroups. He taught at Washington University in St. Louis and the University of Texas in San Antonio (UTSA), and is a recognized speaker at numerous security conferences. He continues to read, write, and research cryptographic security issues.

Chapter 1

Introduction

Cryptography is everywhere. It's in your browsers, your mobile phones, the applications and services you use, and probably in places you don't think about. What was once a technology limited to governments, military, and eventually financial systems is now commonly used in about every industry in almost every application on the planet. Actually, since we now regularly send space probes to other planets and even beyond our own solar system, one might claim that cryptography is a universal practice. And while implementing cryptography might not be rocket science, although its development and analysis is certainly mathematically intense, there are important things to know and understand to deploy good crypto versus bad crypto.

To be clear, cryptanalysis and its underlying math is beyond the scope of this book. And while a little bit of math is unavoidable, it is kept to a minimum. Rather, this book focuses on crypto engineering: the design, implementation, deployment, testing, and assessment of cryptographic architectures. There are many good books on number theory and general cryptography such as the *Handbook of Applied Cryptography* [1] and *Applied Cryptography* [2]. There are also many excellent books on the history of cryptography such as *The Code Book* [3] and *The Code Breakers* [6]. This book provides a basic description of cryptography, protocols, risk management, key management, data management, and security assessments, and offers several illustrations putting all of these various elements into an overall strategy for establishing a cryptographic architecture.

Consider any development or maintenance project. Application developers will typically offer a simple diagram consisting of a few boxes with arrows representing various application systems. Network engineers will often provide a more detailed diagram showing various network connections and components such as routers, firewalls, and datacenters. However, the information security professional is forced to interpret and compare the application and network diagrams and expand the information to address the relevant security controls [4]. One of the more critical aspects of the use of cryptography is to achieve security controls and their associated key management lifecycle controls. This book provides a guide to cryptographic architectures.

1.1 Book Organization

This book and its chapters are organized as follows. Each chapter builds on the previous chapter with the final chapter providing illustrations.

Chapter 1: Introduction provides an overview of the book, cryptographic terminology, and a general discussion of industry groups and standards that define cryptographic algorithms, schemas, protocols, and message specifications. Readers of this book are also presented with a road map for readability of roles and general job descriptions.

Chapter 2: Cryptography Basics presents a synopsis of cryptographic functions including encryption, authentication and integrity, non-repudiation, and tokenization processes. Modern algorithms, key sizes, and relevant security services are discussed. This chapter provides a knowledge foundation for later chapters and also provides crypto reference material.

Chapter 3: Cryptographic Keys reviews symmetric keys, asymmetric private and public key pairs, and public key certificates. This chapter expands the cryptography discussion from the previous chapter and discusses public key infrastructures (PKI) but does not address operational aspects. For details see *Security without Obscurity: A Guide to PKI Operations* [5].

Chapter 4: Authentication Protocols considers several common authentication protocols that rely on cryptography but typically do not address key management issues. Often one or more of these protocols are used within the application or network architectures and thus affect the corresponding cryptographic architecture.

Chapter 5: Security Protocols considers several common security protocols that rely on cryptography but typically do not address key management issues. Often one or more of these protocols are used within the application or network architectures and thus affect the corresponding cryptographic architecture.

Chapter 6: Architectures compares the commonalities and differences between various architectures and introduces the cryptographic architecture. The foundational information provided in the previous chapters is assimilated into the cryptographic architecture. The information needed for documenting a cryptographic architecture is explored along with its characteristics and attributes.

Chapter 7: Risk Management discusses data lifecycle and cryptographic key lifecycle considerations along with the differences between using cryptographic hardware modules versus cryptographic software modules. The relative risks are examined and analyzed.

Chapter 8: Security Assessments provides guidelines on how to conduct a security assessment in order to determine the cryptographic architecture.

Information might come from internal, external, or publicly available sources. Interviews might be internal, external, or adversarial situations. This chapter also explores analysis and reporting.

Chapter 9: Illustrations pulls together all the previous chapters by considering several hypothetical scenarios. These are theoretical case studies intended to demonstrate the information presented in the previous chapters.

1.2 Book Applicability

This book is applicable to system architects, managers, administrators, security professionals, auditors, and even lawyers. These roles range from support staff to senior management including chief information officers, chief technology officers, and chief information security officers. Each can benefit from this book in a variety of ways involving general education and awareness of cryptography and key management issues.

System Architects are responsible for general research, keeping up with technology, making strategic decisions, and assisting others (technology managers, auditors, and security professionals) with making good tactical decisions that improve systems, and operations.

Technology Managers are responsible for making tactical decisions and supervising personnel including administrators and security professionals. The more management understands the underlying technologies supported by their teams, the better they can manage their staff and make superior decisions.

Administrators are responsible for installing, configuring, running, monitoring, and eventually decommissioning network, system, and application components inclusive of hardware devices, firmware modules, and software elements. Basic knowledge of cryptographic architectures is necessary for administrators to properly manage cryptographic features, functionality, and associated cryptographic keys.

Security Professionals are responsible for supporting operational teams, assisting development teams, and managing information security policy, standards, practices, and procedures. But security professionals are often expected to have general knowledge of many areas with expertise typically in only a few areas, so reference material is always a valuable commodity.

Auditors are responsible for verifying compliance to information and security policy, standards, practices, and procedures. Risk can be better identified and managed when the evaluator has a solid understanding of general cryptography and related key management. Further, compliance includes not just the organization's internal security requirements but also external influences such as regulations, international and national laws, and contractual responsibilities.

Corporate Lawyers are responsible for legal practices and interpretations within an organization. Consequently, having a basic understanding of cryptography enhances their ability to provide counsel on technology claims, operational risks, and even privacy issues.

Clearly, others can benefit from this book. Cryptographic architectures provide a means to document what, where, when, why, and how keys are deployed and managed within the context of an application and network deployment. Otherwise, these types of details are typically overlooked or undocumented, and the information, if known, is often lost. The means and methods for determining a cryptographic architecture are explored throughout this book.

1.3 Network Cartoons

When presented with an application solution, the business managers or development team will typically provide a high-level design document; see Figure 1.1. Looking at the figure from left to right, customers access the website server over the Internet, the website server gets services from the application server, and the application server gets data from the database (DB) server.

Viewing the same figure from right to left, administrators log on to the admin server (AS) to manage the various servers including the software server (SS), and the SS pushes updates to the other various servers. Updates might include system software, application software, and configuration data. An information security professional will have many questions regarding data flows, data storage, protection methods, authentication, authorization, and logs. The basic problem is that such a high-level diagram is basically a "cartoon" that conveys very little significant security information.

When pressed for additional information security details, the application managers or developers might provide another high-level design document; see Figure 1.2. Following the figure from left to right, customers access the web server which resides within demilitarized zone (DMZ), the web server connects to App server (AS) which resides on the internal network, and the AS gets data from the DB server. What is new to this diagram is that the web server sits within a DMZ presumably behind at least one external firewall, and communicates to the AS sitting on the internal network, again presumably separated by one or more internal firewalls. Firewall rules are a new element.

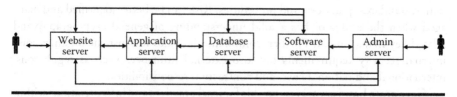

Figure 1.1   Application architecture.

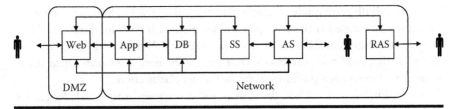

Figure 1.2   Access architecture.

Tracing the figure from right to left, administrators log on to the AS to manage the various servers including the SS, and the SS pushes updates to the other various servers. What is new to this diagram is that administrators have network access to the AS and remote access via the remote access server (RAS). Also, the AS and SS which sit on the internal network both communicate to the web server which resides in the DMZ across the internal firewalls. The information provided by the Access Architecture is helpful, but more information is needed especially with regard to the actual network topology. Thus, the Access Architecture is another "cartoon" without providing sufficient security information. The updated diagram raises more questions than answers.

When pushed for additional information security details, the network team might provide another high-level diagram to include some network information; see Figure 1.3. Looking at the figure from left to right, customers access the web server and administrators connect to the RAS. Both servers are located in the DMZ which is bracketed between the Internet and the internal network by a pair of firewalls. An external router (R) enables access to the DMZ, another router within the DMZ enables access to the internal network, and a third router manages the internal network.

The web server communicates to the AS which connects to the DB server over an application virtual local area network (VLAN) shown as a solid line. Conversely, the RAS communicates to the AS which connects to the SS and other servers over a separate admin VLAN denoted by a dotted line. What is new to this diagram is the network topology of the DMZ and the internal network showing the various routers, firewalls, and the two VLAN separating applications from administration.

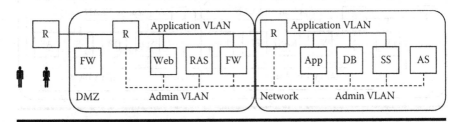

Figure 1.3   Network architecture.

However, this diagram implies a single network instance with all routers, firewalls, and servers comingled at the same physical location with no redundancy, load balancing, or backup capabilities. Hence, the Network Architecture is yet another "cartoon" that provides more information but raises more questions. Once again, an information security professional needs further clarification.

When interviewed further, the system architects reveal the actual design; see Figure 1.4. The Network Architecture is duplicated in two regional datacenters: West and East. The two external routers are cross-connected, such that a connection to the West external router might be redirected to the East external router, and likewise a connection to the East external router might be redirected to the West external router. This cross-connection allows the datacenters to backup each other. Regardless of which external path is chosen the external firewall always interrogates the connection.

Another discovery is the existence of the Business Portal (BP) server which supports an application direct connection. Comparable to the web server which only offers user access, the BP server offers a business-to-business connection for high volume traffic. Similar to the web server, the BP server communicates to the AS which connects to the DB server over the application VLAN. Also, the BP server is accessed by the SS and the AS over the Admin VLAN. As is often the case with enhancement projects, the focus on updating the web and ASs overlooked the BP server as, for this example, no changes are planned.

Another difference is the cross-connection between the Region West and Region East internal network routers. This connection allows data synchronization between the regional servers: ASs, DB servers, SSs, and (ASs). The internal network router

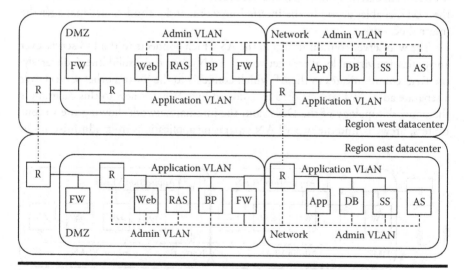

Figure 1.4   Enterprise architecture.

connection also allows system, DB, and application administrators to manage maintenance changes and modifications pushed from either region to another.

The examples discussed in this chapter provide a typical discovery process when an information security professional gets involved with an enhancement project. Incomplete information is usually par as the various project teams have limited experience with information security issues and solutions. However, the importance of maintaining network diagrams should not be ignored nor understated. As an industry example, consider the Payment Card Industry Data Security Standard [24] requirements referring to current (accurate) network diagrams.

∎ 1.1.2 Current network diagram that identifies all connections between the cardholder data environment and other networks, including any wireless networks.

∎ 1.1.3 Current diagram that shows all cardholder data flows across systems and networks.

Further, as another industry example, X9-TR-39 PIN Security and Key Management [28] addresses documented procedures (including network diagrams) within its compliance control objectives.

∎ 4.1.1 Secure Environment for PINs and Keys
The secure environment is physically, logically, and procedurally protected with access controls or other mechanisms designed to prevent any penetration, which would result in the disclosure of all or part of any cryptographic key and/or PINs stored within the environment. Documented procedures exist and are followed that ensure the secured environment remains secure until all keying material has been removed or destroyed.
References X9.8-1—Section 6.3.3 [29]; X9.24-1—Sections 7.3 and 7.5.2 [30]; X9.24-2—Section 7.3 [31].

Consequently, industry standards are equally important. However, technical and security standards abound with abbreviations, nomenclature, and terminology. Accordingly, the reader is provided with a cryptography lexicon and an overview of industry standards.

1.4 Cryptography Lexicon

It was mentioned in the previous section that a little bit of math is unavoidable, but it is kept to a minimum. This section provides a simple math refresher, commonly used notation, and conventional cryptographic terminology used throughout the book. The information is listed by increasing order of difficulty.

Integers	Notation: N is the set of all natural numbers { 1, 2, 3, 4 ...} Notation: Z is the set of all integers {... –3, –2, –1, 0, 1, 2, 3 ...}

Prime
  numbers
	Integers divisible by 1 and itself { 2, 3, 5, 7, 11 ...}
	Note that the integer 1 is not a prime number, the integer
	  2 is the only even prime number as every other even
	  number is divisible by 2, and variables p and q are typically
	  used.

Addition +	Add two integers such as $3 + 2 = 5$. Notation: $x + y = z$
Multiplication *	Multiply two integers such as $3 * 5 = 15$. Notation: $x * y = z$

Math order	Operators within parenthesis are first, then multiplication,
	  then addition such as $(3 + 2) * 3 + 2 = 17$.
	Note that parenthesis can also indicate functions: $F(x) = y$ is
	  read "F of x equals y" where "x" is an input into the
	  function "F" with output "y."

Division
÷
	Divide an integer (the dividend) by another (the divisor) to
	  get an answer in two parts, the quotient and the
	  remainder.
	For example, let 17 be the dividend, 5 be the divisor, so the
	  quotient is 3 with a remainder of 2
	Notation: $17 ÷ 5 = 3$ remainder 2, so $5 * 3 + 2 = 17$
	Notation: $d ÷ v = q$ and r so $v * q + r = d$

Modularity mod	Divide an integer by another (the modulus) to get just the remainder. For example, let 17 be divided by 5 so the remainder is 2. Notations: 17 mod 5 = 2 or 2 = 17 mod 5 Notations: x mod y = z or z = x mod y

Exponentiation	Raise an integer to the power of another, such as $3 * 3 = 9$
	  is three to the power of two (or three squared), and
	  $3 * 3 * 3 = 27$ is three to the power of three (or three
	  cubed).
	Notations: $3^2 = 9$ where 2 is an exponent, $3^3 = 27$ where 3 is
	  an exponent
	Notations: $x^y = z$ or $z = x^y$

Logarithm	The exponent to which an integer (the base) is raised to
	  produce another integer, such as $9 = 3^2$ where 2 is the
	  logarithm of 9 using base 3.
	Notation: y is the logarithm of z using base x for $z = x^y$

(Continued)

Mathematical function	Mathematical function "F" that affects data with an input "x" and an output "y" such as F(x + 2) = y so, for example, if x = 3 then y = 5. Notation: F(x) = y Note that a function can have multiple inputs such as F(x * y) = z so, for example, if x = 3 and y = 5 then z = 15. Notation: F(x, y) = z
Cryptographic function	Mathematical algorithm that affects data using a cryptographic key as one of the inputs: Function (Key, Input) = Output Notations: F(K, I) = O or K(I) = O
Symmetric algorithm	Cryptographic function "F" that uses the same key "K" as for the inverse "F⁻¹" function. Notations: F(K, I) = O and F⁻¹(K,O) = I Other notations: K(I) = O and K(O) = I
Asymmetric algorithm	Cryptographic function "F" that uses different keys "U" and "V" for the inverse "F⁻¹" function. Notations: F(U, I) = O and F⁻¹(V,O) = I Other notations: U(I) = O and V(O) = I
Hash function	Mathematical algorithm that generates a fixed length output from variable length inputs. Notation: H(I) = O
Binary bit	Smallest piece of information limited to values: 0 or 1
Binary nibble	String of four bits with 16 possible values: 0000 0001 0010 0011 0100 0101 0110 0111 1000 1001 1010 1011 1100 1101 1110 1111
Hexadecimal digit	Single digit representing four bits, with 16 possible values: 0, 1, 2, 3, 4, 5, 6, 7, 8, 0, A, B, C, D, E, and F. 0 = 0000 1 = 0001 2 = 0010 3 = 0011 4 = 0100 5 = 0101 6 = 0110 7 = 0111 8 = 1000 9 = 1001 A = 1010 B = 1011 C = 1100 D = 1101 E = 1110 F = 1111 Hexadecimal digits are basically shorthand for writing binary bits. Thus, instead of writing long strings of binary bits, the same value can be written in a fourth number of digits. Further, hexadecimal digits, also called just "hex" are written in groups of four digits, and often lowercase letters (a, b, c, d, e, f) are used instead of uppercase. Notation: ED32 = 1110 1101 0011 0010

(Continued)

Decimal math Base 10	Everyone knows that 237 is two hundred and thirty-seven, but an interesting question is why? The reason is math. Each numeric position from right to left increases the exponential power of the base, times the numeric value for that position. $237 = 2 * 10^2 + 3 * 10^1 + 7 * 10^0$ $237 = 2 * 100 + 3 * 10 + 7 * 1$ $237 = 200 + 30 + 7$ This is an important concept because other base values besides 10 can be used, which is why binary and hexadecimal also work, and also why each hexadecimal digit represents four binary bits.
Binary math Base 2	The decimal value 237 is 1110 1101 in binary notation. Unlike decimal math which has 10 characters (0, 1, 2, 3, 4, 5, 6, 7, 8, and 9) binary math only has two characters (0 and 1). $237 = 1 * 2^7 + 1 * 2^6 + 1 * 2^5 + 0 * 2^4 + 1 * 2^3 + 1 * 2^2 + 0 * 2^1 + 1 * 2^0$ $237 = 1 * 128 + 1 * 64 + 1 * 32 + 0 * 16 + 1 * 8 + 1 * 4 + 0 * 2 + 1 * 1$ $237 = 128 + 64 + 32 + 0 + 8 + 4 + 0 + 1$ Thus, the binary string represents the same decimal value.
Hexadecimal math Base 16	The decimal value 237 is ED in hex notation. Unlike decimal math which has 10 characters (0, 1, 2, 3, 4, 5, 6, 7, 8, and 9) hex math has 16 characters (0, 1, 2, 3, 4, 5, 6, 7, 8, 9, A, B, C, D, E, and F). $237 = E * 16^1 + D * 16^0$ $237 = E * 16 + D * 1$ and in decimal $14 * 16 + 13 * 1$ $237 = 224 + 13$ Thus, the hex string represents the same decimal value.
Tridecimal math Base 13	The decimal value 54 is 42 in tridecimal notation. $54 = 4 * 13^1 + 2 * 13^0$ $54 = 4 * 13 + 2 * 1$ $54 = 52 + 2$ So the real answer to the question "what is 9 * 6?" really is 42 if you think like a pan-dimensional being in base 13 math. Just saying.…

(Continued)

Exclusive OR ⊕	Bit-wise operation that has two bits as input and one bit as output:
	$$0 \oplus 0 = 0$$ $$0 \oplus 1 = 1$$ $$1 \oplus 0 = 1$$ $$1 \oplus 1 = 1$$
	Exclusive OR (symbol ⊕ also denoted XOR) yields a 0 if the two bits have the same value (0, 0) or (1, 1) and a 1 if the two bits have different values (1, 0) or (0, 1). This simple binary function is a very powerful and common cryptographic tool. XOR can be applied to hex digits since a hex digit is a shorthand notation for binary bits. For example:
	$$1010 \oplus 0110 = 1100 \text{ is } A \oplus 6 = C$$
	See Annex: XOR Quick Reference for a complete list of XOR values in hex and binary.
Base64 Encoding	Cryptographic data is not always encoded using binary or hexadecimal formats because some values are not displayable while others might be interpreted by systems as control characters or commands and cause unwanted results.
	For example, the American Standard Code for Information Interchange (ASCII pronounced "ass-ski") is a 7-bit encoding scheme used by most small to medium computer systems. ASCII includes system commands recognized by many computers such as line feeds and carriage returns.
	As another example, the Extended Binary Coded Decimal Interchange Code (EBCDIC pronounced "ebb-sih-dick") is an 8-bit encoding scheme used by mainframe computers. EBCDIC also includes system commands recognized by computers.
	See the Annex: ASCII and EBCDIC Quick Reference for details.
	Thus, for non-display characters and especially for cryptographic data, the bits are often encoded using Base64 which is a 6-bit encoding scheme that provides data transparency. Binary bits are first converted to Base64 encoded human readable characters that computer systems will ignore. The readable characters are then safely transmitted via email or file transfer protocols. Once received, the Base64 encoded characters can then be converted back to binary bits.
	See the Annex: Base64 Quick Reference for details.

The reader is now armed with sufficient math notation and cryptographic terminology used throughout the book. Another area the reader should familiarize themselves is industry standards and the standard developer organizations.

1.5 Industry Standards

Reading books, technical papers, journal articles, and blogs can be informational and often instructional, but knowing and understanding industry standards and specifications is a treasure trove. Cryptographic algorithms, schemas, protocols, and message specifications are all defined in standards. It is also important to understand who developed which standard. Figure 1.5 shows an overview of relevant standards organizations, including national standards body (NSB) and standards development organization (SDO) groups.

International Standards Organization[*] (ISO) develops numerous worldwide standards based on consensus with 163 participating member countries. ISO is organized into hundreds of technical committees (TCs) arranged by industry areas that have published over 21,000 international standards and related documents. For example, TC1 is screw threads, TC120 is leather, TC215 is health informatics, and TC307 is blockchain and distributed ledger technologies. Relevant to this book is TC68 for financial services.

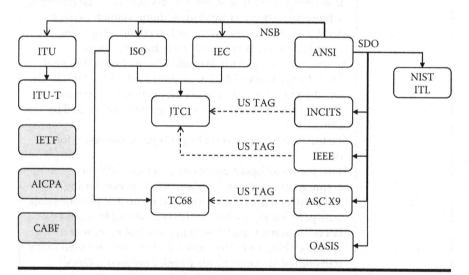

Figure 1.5   Standards organizations.

---

[*] www.iso.org

Members* of ISO are countries with NSB; individuals or companies cannot become ISO members. ISO offers three membership categories (full, correspondent, and subscriber) to over 160 countries, including the following:

- The Australian NSB is Standards Australia† (SA)
- The Canadian NSB is the Standards Council of Canada‡ (SCC)
- The French NSB is the Association French Normalization Organization Regulation§ (AFNOR)
- The German NSB is the Deutsches Institut für Normung¶ (DIN)
- The Japanese NSB is the Japanese Industrial Standards Committee** (JISC)
- The United Kingdom's NSB is the British Standards Institution†† (BSI)
- The United States' NSB is the American National Standards Institute (ANSI)

International Electrotechnical Commission‡‡ (IEC) develops worldwide standards for electrical, electronic, and related technologies (known collectively as "electrotechnology") based on consensus with 83 participating member countries and over 2,000 industry experts. IEC is organized into over 100 TCs and cooperates with ISO and International Telecommunication Union (ITU) by means of joint committees. Relevant to this book is the ISO/IEC Joint Technical Committee One (JTC1) for information technology.

International Telecommunication Union§§ (ITU) is the United Nations specialized agency for information and communication technologies. The ITU study group Telecommunication Standardization Sector (ITU-T) develops worldwide standards (called ITU-T Recommendations) based on consensus with 176 member countries. ITU-T is organized into 11 active study groups. Relevant to this book is the ITU-T study group SG17 for Security.

Note that the ITU-T offers many of its standards¶¶ for free.

ISO, IEC, and ITU-T are basically the three pillars for international standardization. Membership is at the country level where each country has a designated NSB. Each country's NSB is responsible as the technical advisory group (TAG), but this can be delegated to other groups accredited by the NSB as an SDO.

---

* ISO Standards Bodies: www.iso.org/members.html
† www.standards.org.au/Pages/default.aspx
‡ www.scc.ca/
§ www.afnor.org/
¶ www.din.de/de
** www.jisc.go.jp/
†† www.bsigroup.com/
‡‡ www.iec.ch
§§ www.itu.int
¶¶ www.itu.int/ITU-T/recommendations/index.aspx

American National Standards Institution* (ANSI) is the NSB for the United States. ANSI does not develop standards per se but rather accredits other SDO per various industry segments and assigns them as US TAG to ISO, IEC, or ITU committees. ANSI currently has accredited 282 SDO and assigned 584 TAG to various ISO TCs and subcommittees. Relevant to this book are SDOs' National Institute of Standards and Technology (NIST), International Committee for Information Technology Standards (INCITS), Accredited Standards Committee X9 (ASC X9), Organization for the Advancement of Structured Information Standards (OASIS), and Institute of Electrical and Electronics Engineers (IEEE).

National Institute of Standards and Technology† (NIST) is a US government agency that promotes innovation and industrial competitiveness by advancing measurement science, standards, and technology. Within the NIST organization, the Information Technology Laboratory (ITL) is an ANSI SDO. However, NIST also produces its own Federal Information Processing Standards (FIPS) Publications and Special Publication. Relevant to this book are several FIPS and Special Publications numbered from the 800 series.

International Committee for Information Technology Standards‡ (INCITS) is an ANSI-accredited SDO and the TAG to ISO/IEC JTC1 with 500 participating member organizations. INCITS was originally named the *Accredited Standards Committee X3* from 1961 to 1996, and currently has eight TCs and manages over a dozen TAG relationships with various ISO committee and JTC1 subcommittees. For example, INCITS is the TAG to Technical Committee 307 blockchain and distributed ledger. Relevant to this book are TCs B10 Identification Cards and Related Devices, CS1 Cyber Security, and M1 Biometrics.

Institute of Electrical and Electronics Engineers§ (IEEE) pronounced "Eye-triple-E" is an ANSI-accredited SDO and TAG to ISO/IEC JTC1 subcommittees with more than 423,000 individuals from more than 160 countries. Relevant to this book is the Technical Committee on Security and Privacy.

Accredited Standards Committee X9¶ (ASC X9) is an ANSI-accredited SDO, the TAG to ISO TC68, and the TC68 secretariat with 112 participating member organizations. X9 has five active subcommittees and manages several TAG relationships with TC68 subcommittees. Relevant to this book is the X9F Information Security subcommittee with its three active workgroups: X9F1 Cryptographic Tools, X9F4 Cryptographic Protocols and Application Security, and X9F6 Cardholder Authentication and Integrated Circuit Chip (ICC).

---

* www.ansi.org
† www.nist.gov
‡ www.incits.org
§ www.ieee.org
¶ www.x9.org

Organization for the Advancement of Structured Information Standards[*] (OASIS) is an ANSI-accredited SDO with over 600 participating member organizations. OASIS was originally named *SGML Open* from 1993 to 1998, and currently manages seven-member sections with 65 active TCs. Relevant to this book are TCs Key Management Interoperability Protocol, PKCS 11, and Security Assertion Markup Language (SAML) Services.

Internet Engineering Task Force[†] (IETF) is a stand-alone standards organization unaffiliated with any international or national standards organization. IETF membership is open to any individual who can participate in any of the 138 current working groups organized into seven topic areas. Relevant to this book is the Security Area with its 16 active working groups and some of its 59 concluded groups.

American Institute of Certified Public Accountants[‡] (AICPA) is a stand-alone standards organization unaffiliated with any international or national standards organization. The AICPA is a professional organization for national Certified Public Accountants (CPA) providing rules, standards for auditing private companies and other CPA services, advocacy, educational materials, manages examination, and handles compliance. Relevant to this book are Authoritative Standards Publications.

Certification Authority Browser Forum[§] (CAB Forum) is a stand-alone quasi-standards organization unaffiliated with any international or national standards organization. The CAB Forum is a voluntary group of leading certification authorities (CAs) and vendors of Internet browser software and other applications to define best security practices for Internet transactions and creating a more intuitive method of displaying secure sites to Internet users. Relevant to this book are the basic CA requirements and extended validation guidelines.

The various standards published by these organizations are referenced throughout the book as needed and typically left as additional research for the reader. However, standards continually evolve, sometimes become obsolete, and other times are replaced by other standards, so the reader needs to verify which version of a standard is being used. Some organizations such as ISO and ANSI require reaffirmations or updates at least every five years but keep the same number and only revise the publication dates. Other organizations such as IETF update standards as needed and change the number to the next available designation.

---

[*] www.oasis-open.org
[†] www.ietf.org
[‡] www.aicpa.org
[§] www.cabforum.org

Chapter 2

Cryptography Basics

Cryptographers are mathematicians who specialize in cryptography or cryptanalysis. Essentially, cryptanalysis is breaking protection mechanisms, whereas cryptography is making protection mechanisms. All cryptographers are mathematicians but not all mathematicians are cryptographers. This book includes some math and discusses some cryptographic concepts but does not use any serious math.

- Cryptography is from the Greek words "kyrptós" meaning hidden (or secret) and "graphein" meaning writing.
- Cryptanalysis is from the Greek words "kyrptós" meaning hidden (or secret) and "analýein" meaning loosen (or untie).

The first known use of cryptography was in ancient Egypt [6] when the priesthood substituted common hieroglyphics with secret symbols to hide their true meaning. Governments and military have used cryptography for thousands of years for secret communications. Modern cryptography and cryptanalysis began during World War II with the infamous German Enigma* machine and the Japanese Purple cipher. The financial services industry has been using cryptography for decades to protect personal identification numbers with automated teller machines and point-of-sale terminals. Information technology uses various types of cryptography to protect communications, passwords, files, databases, and much more.

For the purposes of this book, cryptography is discussed as symmetric versus asymmetric methods, and organized into encryption, integrity and authentication, non-repudiation, and tokenization services. There are many associated topics such as random numbers, prime numbers, exclusive OR, hashing, and many other functions referenced in this book but only as they pertain to cryptographic

---

* www.bbc.co.uk/history/topics/enigma

architectures. Some of the notation used in this chapter includes the following abbreviations and acronyms.

DH	Diffie–Hellman
DSA	Digital Signature Algorithm
ECDSA	Elliptic Curve Digital Signature Algorithm
ECDH	Elliptic Curve Diffie–Hellman
HMAC	Keyed Hash Message Authentication Code
ICV	Integrity Check Value
MAC	Message Authentication Code
PKC	Public Key Cryptography
RSA	Rivest–Shamir–Adleman
XOR	Exclusive OR

Cryptography, like mathematics, is an evolving science. What might have been considered secure or good practices today can change and become obsolete or vulnerable. Mathematical problems once considered difficult enough for cryptographic use have and will continue to get resolved such that better and stronger algorithms are always needed. Scientific research in physics and quantum computers will continue to increase computational capabilities such that strong algorithms eventually become weak and need to be replaced. Meanwhile, the fundamental principles in this book remain valid and continue to be valuable.

2.1 Encryption

Encryption provides data confidentiality, either in storage or during transmission. In general, the encryption process transforms data from cleartext to ciphertext using a cryptographic key such that any party without access to the key cannot reverse the process. However, encryption does not provide data integrity, as the ciphertext can still be altered rendering the decrypted data useless. See Section 2.3 for a discussion on data integrity and authentication.

Symmetric encryption is depicted in Figure 2.1 showing cleartext transformed into ciphertext and back into cleartext. The same key is used to encrypt and to decrypt, hence the term "symmetric" cryptography, sometimes called "secret key" to distinguish symmetric keys from asymmetric keys. Following the data path in Figure 2.1 from left to right, the cleartext and key are inputs into the encrypt

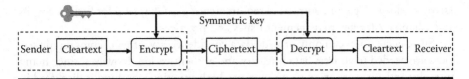

Figure 2.1 Symmetric encryption.

function which yields the ciphertext. The ciphertext and the same key are inputs into the decrypt function which recovers the original cleartext.

When a sender and receiver are involved, as noted with dotted boxes, the sender encrypts the cleartext and transmits the ciphertext to the receiver. The receiver uses the same key to decrypt the ciphertext for recovering the cleartext. In this manner, any third party attempting to access the transmitted data can only "see" the ciphertext and is unable to read the cleartext. Thus, only the sender and receiver who have access to the key can access the cleartext. However, if the sender or receiver shares the key with other parties, the overall system security can be weakened. See Chapter 3 for further details and Chapter 7 for key management issues and practices.

Asymmetric encryption is illustrated in Figure 2.2 showing cleartext transformed into ciphertext and back into cleartext but using different keys to encrypt and decrypt. Asymmetric keys always come in pairs, where one key is called the public key and the other private key. Following the data path from left to right, the cleartext and public key are inputs into the encrypt function which yields the ciphertext. The ciphertext and private key are inputs into the decrypt function which recovers the original cleartext. Cleartext encrypted using the public key cannot be decrypted using the public key, only the corresponding private key will work.

When a sender and receiver are involved, as noted with dotted boxes, the sender encrypts the cleartext using the receiver's public key and transmits the ciphertext to the receiver. The receiver uses the corresponding private key to decrypt the ciphertext to recover the cleartext. Thus, only the receiver who has access to the private key can decrypt the data. The sender already has access to the cleartext. In general, anyone who has the receiver's public key can encrypt data, but only the receiver who has the private key can decrypt the data. Asymmetric key pair owners should never share the private key, although keys might be backed up for recovery or

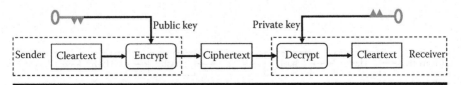

Figure 2.2 Asymmetric encryption.

escrowed due to legal or contractual requirements. See Chapter 3 for further details and Chapter 7 for key management issues and practices.

Since encryption can only provide data confidentiality, other cryptographic services are needed to address data integrity and authentication. However, since many integrity and authentication techniques use hash functions, hashing is discussed in Section 2.2.

2.2 Hash Functions

Hash functions are shown in Figure 2.3, but note that hashing is not necessarily a cryptographic function; hash functions do not use cryptographic keys. Rather, many cryptographic methods employ hash functions. But not all hash functions are good enough to be used with cryptographic methods; a sufficiently strong hash is called a cryptographic hash. The basic hash process is to input the cleartext into a hash function whose output is a hash value, often just called a hash. We denote the hash function as $H(C) = h$ where uppercase "H" is the hash function, uppercase "C" is the input cleartext, and lowercase "h" is the output. Any hash function inputs a variable length cleartext but outputs a fixed length hash.

Hashes are also called "one-way" functions because given a hash the function cannot be reversed to recover the cleartext; hashing is irreversible. The purpose of the hash is a relatively unique representation, sometimes called a fingerprint, of the cleartext. The hash is "relatively" unique because the total number of possible inputs (variable length cleartext) is much larger than the number of possible outputs (fixed length hash). This simply means that multiple cleartext inputs may yield the same hash. So for some set of different cleartext (C_i, C_j, C_k, or more), the same hash function yields the same hash: so $H(C_i) = H(C_j) = H(C_k) = h$. This is called a hash collision which is characteristic of any hash function. However, some hash functions have collision rates that are too high; this is the fundamental reason for cryptographic hash algorithms.

Cryptographic hash algorithms have three essential characteristics.

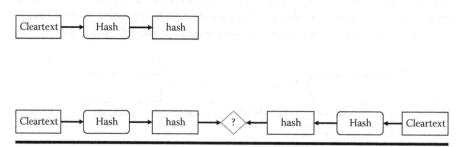

Figure 2.3   Hash function.

- **Pre-image resistance**: given a hash value (h) it is difficult to find any cleartext (Ci) such that H(Ci) = h. This characteristic is the basis for a one-way function.
- **Second pre-image resistance**: given an input cleartext (Ci) it is difficult to find another cleartext (Cj) such that H(Ci) = H(Cj).
- **Collision resistance**: it is difficult to find any two cleartext (Cj) and (Ck) such that H(Cj) = H(Ck). The pair (Cj) and (Ck) is called a cryptographic hash collision.

Older hash functions such as MD4 and MD5 (named for message digest, another term for hash value) with 128-bit hashes are no longer considered cryptographically secure. Federal Information Processing Standard (FIPS) 180-4 [28] defines the Secure Hash Algorithm SHA-1 with 160-bit hash as a replacement for earlier message digest algorithms; SHA-2 family with 224-bit, 256-bit, 384-bit, and 512-bit hashes as a replacement for SHA-1. FIPS 202 [29] introduces an alternative SHA-3 family with 224-bit, 256-bit, 384-bit, and 512-bit hashes as a future replacement for SHA-2. Since SHA-2 is a family of hash algorithms, they are often referred to as SHA-256 or SHA-512; however, since the SHA-2 and SHA-3 have the same sizes, the hash algorithms can be confusing.

Hash algorithms are used to protect stored passwords, as a type of non-cryptographic checksum, or with cryptographic keys discussed in Section 2.3. However, hash functions are susceptible to exhaustive attacks. Knowing the hash algorithm in use, anyone can create a list, commonly called a rainbow table, of possible hash values based on likely cleartext. For example, a hash table of all possible social security numbers (SSNs) is feasible since every possible SSN is also known. As another example, creating a rainbow table of all possible passwords is more difficult; however, generating a smaller table of commonly used 8-character passwords is much easier. Further, it is equally likely that such rainbow tables already exist.

2.3 Integrity and Authentication

There are several data integrity and authentication methods including MAC and HMAC. In general, an ICV is created from the cleartext using a cryptographic key such that any party without access to the key cannot recreate the ICV. Any change to the cleartext is discernable because the ICV would not verify. However, data integrity and authentication do not provide data confidentially, as the cleartext is needed to create and verify the ICV. See Section 2.1 for a discussion on data confidentiality.

- MAC [7] encrypts the cleartext but only retains part of the ciphertext as an ICV.
- HMAC [8] merges (XOR) the cleartext with a key and hashes the result as an ICV.

Symmetric integrity and authentication is illustrated in Figure 2.4 showing cleartext and a key used to create an ICV which can be verified using the same cleartext and key. The same key is used to create and verify the ICV, thus "symmetric" cryptography can provide data integrity and authentication. Following the data path from left to right, the cleartext and key are inputs to the MAC (or HMAC) function which yields the ICV. The same cleartext and key are inputs to another MAC (or HMAC) function which gives another ICV. If the two ICV match then the cleartext has not been modified or substituted. However, if the two ICV do not match then the cleartext has been altered or replaced.

When a sender and a receiver are involved, as noted with dotted boxes, the sender generates the ICV using the cleartext and sends both the cleartext and ICV to the receiver. The receiver uses the same key to generate another ICV using the cleartext and compares the two ICV. If the two ICV match then the receiver not only knows the cleartext has integrity, the cleartext is also authenticated because only the sender should have the key. However, if the sender or receiver shares the key with other parties, authentication is no longer provided by the ICV. Further, neither the sender nor receiver can claim non-repudiation because the authentication is not provable to a third party. Any third party such as a judge or arbitrator would be unable to determine which party generated the ICV as both, the sender and receiver, has the same capability.

Asymmetric integrity and authentication is depicted in Figure 2.5 showing cleartext and a private key used to create an ICV which can be verified using the corresponding public key. Only the private key can generate the ICV and only the associated public key can verify the ICV, thus "asymmetric" cryptography can provide data integrity with strong authentication. Following the data path from

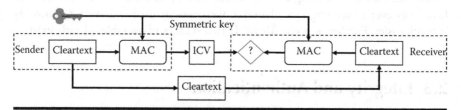

Figure 2.4   Symmetric integrity and authentication.

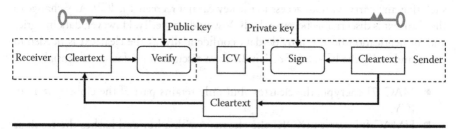

Figure 2.5   Asymmetric integrity and authentication.

right to left (note the reversed asymmetric encryption flow from Section 2.1), the cleartext and private key are inputs to the sign function which yields the ICV (more commonly known as a digital signature). The same cleartext and associated public key are inputs to the verify function. If the digital signature (ICV) verifies then the cleartext has not been modified or substituted, then the signature must have been generated by the corresponding private key.

When a sender and a receiver are involved, as noted with dotted boxes (note the reversed symmetric sender and receiver from Figure 2.4), the sender generates the digital signature using the cleartext and the private key and sends both the cleartext and the digital signature to the receiver. The receiver uses the same cleartext and associated public key to verify the digital signature, and if the signature verifies the receiver not only knows the cleartext has integrity, the cleartext has strong authentication because only the sender has the private key. Further, if the sender has the appropriate controls for the private key and digital signature, the receiver might also claim non-repudiation. See Section 2.4 for details of non-repudiation services.

In summary, symmetric algorithms use the same key for:

■ encryption versus decryption, or
■ generation of an ICV for sending a message versus verifying a message.

Conversely, asymmetric algorithms use different keys for:

■ public key for encryption versus private key for decryption, or
■ private key for generation of a digital signature versus public key for verification of a digital signature.

Data confidentiality is provided using encryption. Data integrity and authentication is provided using MAC or HMAC, but both are reputable. Digital signatures provide data integrity with strong authentication and with appropriate controls potentially provide non-repudiation. However, any use of cryptographic keys necessitates that keys be managed is a secure manner to prevent misuse, unauthorized access, and generally avoid key compromise. For more information regarding the key management life cycle, see Chapter 3.

2.4 Non-Repudiation

Non-Repudiation is the set of controls necessary to prevent repudiation, which is the refusal by one party to acknowledge an agreement claimed by another party. As discussed in *Security without Obscurity: A Guide to Confidentiality, Authentication, and Integrity* [4], there are technical, cryptographic, operational, and legal considerations. Technology considerations include two primary industry elements.

- Extended Validation (EV) certificates; see the CA/Browser Forum's Guidelines for Extended Validation Certificates [16]. EV certificates require additional subject authentication and authorization procedures performed by the Registration Authority (RA) and the Certification Authority (CA). The historical origin behind EV certificates was an attempt to address an industry challenge of invalid certificates. The CA (and RA) is audited to the EV criteria and recognized as issuing EV certificates versus regular certificate. An EV-designated CA cannot issue regular certificate just as a regular CA cannot issue EV certificates. However, EV certificate do not mystically provide digital signatures with non-repudiation properties.
- Certificate key usage "non-repudiation" flag, which has been renamed to "content commitment" to avoid confusion; see Annex: X.509 Certificate Quick Reference. However, the presence of the flag does not magically manifest non-repudiation.

Rather, each of the public key infrastructure (PKI) participants needs to provide the appropriate cryptographic, operational, and legal controls. Cryptographic considerations begin with digital signature algorithms. There are numerous digital signature algorithms based on asymmetric algorithms. Some of the algorithms are named for inventors, whereas others are abbreviations.

- RSA is named for its inventors Ron Rivest,[*] Adi Shamir,[†] and Leonard Adleman[‡] based on the ground breaking 1978 paper [9] and codified in the American National Standards Institute (ANSI) standard [10].
- DSA is named the Digital Signature Algorithm codified in the NIST standard [11].
- ECDSA is named the Elliptic Curve Digital Signature Algorithm codified in the ANSI standard [12].

Asymmetric digital signatures are depicted in Figure 2.6 showing cleartext and a private key used to create a digital signature (called an ICV in Section 2.3) which can be verified using the associated public key encapsulated in a digital certificate [13]. Only the private key can generate the digital signature and only the associated public key can verify the signature. Following the data path from right to left, the cleartext and private keys are inputs into the sign function which yields the digital signature. The same cleartext and associated public key are inputs into the verify function. If the digital signature verifies then the cleartext has data integrity, and the digital signature provides strong authentication.

---

[*] http://people.csail.mit.edu/rivest/
[†] http://amturing.acm.org/award_winners/shamir_2327856.cfm
[‡] www.cs.usc.edu/people/faculty/tenured-tenure-track-faculty/adleman-leonard

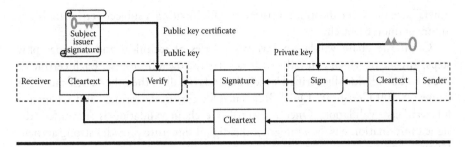

Figure 2.6   Digital signature.

The digital certificate, sometimes called a public key certificate, is an identity credential which contains the public key, the asymmetric key pair owner name, the certification authority (CA) name that issued the certificate, and other significant information. The difference emphasized between an ICV and a digital signature is the PKI required to support digital certificates. However, this book is not a guideline [5] on operating a PKI but rather provides sufficient details on managing certificates and the corresponding private keys. See Chapter 3 for more information regarding cryptographic keys.

When a sender and a receiver are involved, as noted with dotted boxes, the sender generates the digital signature using the cleartext and the private key. The sender transmits the cleartext and the signature to the receiver. The receiver uses the same cleartext and associated public key certificate to verity the digital signature. The verification process varies depending on which digital signature algorithm (RSA, DSA, and ECDSA) is being used. Other digital signature algorithms exist and clearly more will be invented as time unfolds but for the purposes of this book only these three digital signature algorithms are referenced.

When the digital signature verifies, the receiver knows the cleartext has data integrity, the sender is authenticated, and theoretically since only the sender controls the corresponding private key, the receiver has the cryptographic foundation for non-repudiation. However, signature verification is not enough, rather certificate validation is needed. Figure 2.7 illustrates a basic certificate chain within any PKI beginning on the left with the subject certificate and ending on the right with the trust anchor. The subject certificate links to the issuer CA certificate, which links to the subordinate CA (sub-CA) certificate, which links to the root CA (trust anchor) certificate. Some PKI might have fewer certificates, whereas

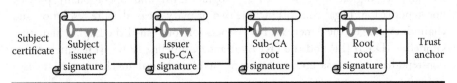

Figure 2.7   Public key infrastructure.

others have more certificates, but three-tier PKI issuing a subject certificate is not an uncommon hierarchy.

Certificate chain validation involves a series of technical and cryptographic steps, anyone of which can fail which negates the overall process. Each certificate needs to be individually verified which depends on all of the other certificates. See Annex: X.509 Certificate Quick Reference for certificate formats and Chapter 3 for certificate validation. Once the certificate chain validation is successful, the signed information has data integrity, the digital signature provides strong authentication, and since only the signer has access to the private key, the integrity and authentication is provable to a third party. However, in addition to the technical and cryptographic steps already discussed, operational and legal controls need to be in place for genuine non-repudiation services.

Operational controls consists of each PKI participant performing according to an agreed-upon set of rules to establish trust. Within any PKI are the following participants:

■ Subject is the entity whose public key and common name are encapsulated within a certificate and who securely manages the corresponding private key. The subject maintains information security controls over its system components such that access controls are in place and system patches are kept current to avoid risks of known vulnerabilities.

■ RA is the entity responsible for authenticating and authorizing subjects, but the RA does not issue or revoke certificates. The RA maintains information security controls over its systems and personnel such that only authorized processes or individuals have access to data and organizational resources.

■ CA is an entity trusted to issue and revoke certificates and depends on an RA to authenticate and authorize the subject. The CA maintains information security controls over its systems and personnel such that only authorized processes or individuals have access to data and organizational resources.

■ Relying Party is the entity who uses the subject certificate and therefore depends on the RA to authenticate and authorize the subject, depends on the CA to issue and revoke certificates, and depends on the subject to securely manage its corresponding private key.

If each PKI participant performs to expectations, especially if the subject securely manages its private key and the relying party performs certificate validation, then the subject's digital signature can cryptographically and operationally provide non-repudiation. Legal controls include two primary areas: dispute resolution and chain of evidence. The American Bar Association* published the Digital Signature Guideline (DSG) [14] and the PKI Assurance Guideline (PAG) [15] which define non-repudiation not as an automatic result of technical mechanisms, but as a

---

* www.americanbar.org

property that can only be determined after recourse to available dispute mechanisms such as a court or arbitrator. The PAG also discusses how the proponent of evidence produced by a digitally signed transaction or communication might seek its admission at trial or another proceeding under established rules of evidence. Basically, all of the cryptographic and operational controls need to be provable to an independent third party.

One method for assuring the RA and CA are operating according to industry standards is an independent audit conducted by an information security professional. The evaluation criteria for such audits are demonstrated by the Webtrust for CA [17] which is recognized by many CA and browser manufacturers who are members of the CA/Browser Forum.* The original Webtrust for CA v1.0 was based on X9.79 [19] which was later internationalized as ISO 21188 [20]. Further, the former PKI Forum, now incorporated into the Organization for the Advancement of Structured Information Standards Identity and Trusted Infrastructure[†] (IDtrust) section, also endorsed the Webtrust audit in its CA Trust [18] white paper. The Webtrust for CA v2.0 audit criteria is currently organized into seven areas:

1. CA Business Practices Disclosures, which are expected to be documented in the CA certificate policy or certificate practices statement.
2. CA Business Practices Management, which are effective controls to provide reasonable assurance that the CA operates according to its certificate policy or practices statement.
3. CA Environmental Controls, which are controls addressing assets, personnel, physical and logical access controls, development, maintenance, monitoring, and security logs.
4. CA Key Life Cycle Management Controls, which address key generation, key storage, key backup and recovery, public key distribution, key usage, key archival, key destruction, key compromise, cryptographic hardware security modules, and key escrow.
5. Subscriber Key Lifecycle Management Controls, which address CA services provided to subscribers for managing users' cryptographic keys.
6. Certificate Lifecycle Management Controls, addressing subscriber registration, certificate renewal, certificate rekey, certificate issuance, certificate distribution, certificate revocation, certificate suspension, and certificate validation. Regarding subscriber registration, refer to EV certificate [16] historical origin discussed previously.
7. Subordinate CA Certificate Lifecycle Management Controls, addressing controls over one or more subordinate CA operating within the hierarchy of a PKI.

---

* https://cabforum.org/
† www.oasis-idtrust.org/

Each of these areas includes control objectives for measuring compliance and illustrative controls as examples, but the Webtrust for CA is neither prescriptive nor proscriptive relative to technology or solutions. Likewise, industry standards [20] define requirements but do not specify technology. Thus, the reader is provided guidance but not the particulars specifications. For a more thorough discussion of PKI operations, refer to Ref. [5], and for a description of these areas relative to this book, refer to Chapter 7.

One last note on digital signatures versus electronic signatures is as follows: the Electronic Signatures in Global and National Commerce Act* (ESIGN) of 2000 [21] defines an electronic signature as an electronic sound, symbol, or process, attached to or logically associated with a contract or other record and executed or adopted by a person with the intent to sign the record. Thus, since a digital signature is a cryptographic process representing the intent to sign a record, it is suitable for an electronic signature. However, without the cryptographic, operational, and legal controls, an electronic signature cannot provide non-repudiation services as described in the DSG and the PAG.

2.5 Tokenization

Tokenization is the process for substituting sensitive data with benign data. Exactly what constitutes sensitive data, also called the underlying sensitive value (USV), is relative to the business application. Generally for payment applications, the account number is sensitive.

For example, the Payment Card Industry Data Security Standard (PCI DSS) Tokenization Guidelines [26] offer an application-specific description: *Tokenization is a process by which the primary account number (PAN) is replaced with a surrogate value called a "token." Detokenization is the reverse process of redeeming a token for its associated PAN value. The security of an individual token relies predominantly on the infeasibility of determining the original PAN knowing only the surrogate value.*

Europay-MasterCard-Visa (EMV) Payment Tokenization Specification [27] offers a similar description: *Payment Tokens are surrogate values that replace the PAN in the payments ecosystem. Payment Tokens may be used to originate payment transactions, whereas non-Payment Tokens may be used for ancillary processes, such as loyalty tracking.*

For health care, the patient's name or diagnostic codes might be deemed sensitive. Regarding privacy, any personally identifiable information such as a mailing address or SSN might be considered sensitive (USV) data that needs protection.

What comprises benign data depends on the tokenization method. X9.119-1 [22] defines requirements for protecting sensitive payment card data using encryption methods, whereas X9.119-2 [23] addresses tokenization methods. X9.119-2 offers

---

* www.gpo.gov/fdsys/pkg/PLAW-106publ229/pdf/PLAW-106publ229.pdf

a similar tokenization definition: *the process of mapping a plaintext value (i.e., the USV) to an existing or newly generated surrogate value (i.e., a token)* and identifies four tokenization methods.

- Encryption method
- MAC method
- Random method
- Table method

Figure 2.8 depicts the tokenization encryption method. The tokenization process is when the USV is encrypted using a symmetric key which results in the token. The detokenization process is when the token is decrypted using the same symmetric key which recovers the USV. Since the USV can be recovered directly from the token no USV database, also called a token vault, is needed. However, the cryptographic key, also called a token key, must be managed securely otherwise if the key is compromised then any token ever generated can be decrypted. Further, unauthorized access to the detokenization service allows recovery of any USV from a token, and unlimited access to the tokenization service allows its misuse to create an exhaustive list, sometimes called a rainbow table, of all possible USV and tokens.

Figure 2.9 shows the tokenization MAC method. The tokenization process is when the USV is used as input into MAC or HMAC function using a symmetric key which results in the token. The detokenization process can only occur using a token vault which contains a mapping of the USV to the token. Alternatively, an USV can be verified with a specific token. Likewise, the token key must be managed securely otherwise if the key is compromised then it can be used to create a rainbow table of all possible USV and tokens. Further, unauthorized access to the detokenization service (if a vault is enabled) allows recovery of any USV from a token, and unlimited access to the tokenization or verification service allows misuse to create a dictionary table of all possible USV and tokens.

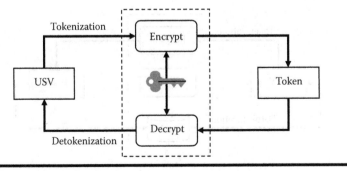

Figure 2.8   Tokenization encryption method.

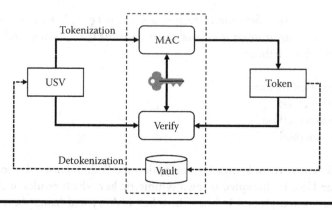

Figure 2.9 Tokenization MAC method.

Figure 2.10 illustrates the tokenization random method. The tokenization process is when the USV is replaced by a random value using a random number generator (RNG). The entropy source for the RNG is independent from the USV input such that the token has no correlation with the USV. Consequently, the detokenization process can only occur using a token vault which contains a mapping of the USV to the token. Additionally, since the random method does not employ a cryptographic key there are no risks due to key compromise; however, the RNG might be influenced to produce skewed versus random values. Further, unauthorized access to the detokenization vault allows recovery of any USV from a token, and unlimited access to the tokenization service allows misuse to create a dictionary table of all possible USV and tokens.

Figure 2.11 shows the tokenization table method. The tokenization process is when the USV is replaced by a value derived from a table of pseudo random numbers. The table is generated once, using an RNG to seed a pseudo random number generator (PRNG) which is used to populate the table. Once generated the table remain static for all tokenization and detokenization. The detokenization process is when the token is replaced by the USV derived from the same table; essentially

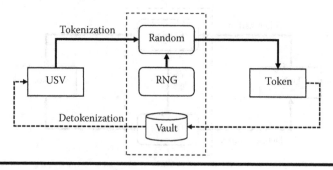

Figure 2.10 Tokenization random method.

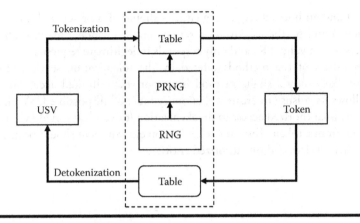

Figure 2.11   Tokenization table method.

tokenization is a lookup, and detokenization is a reverse lookup. Consequently, a token vault is unnecessary. Additionally, since the table method does not employ a cryptographic key there are no risks due to key compromise; however, the RNG or PRNG might be influenced to adversely affect the table. Also, once generated the table needs to be managed securely otherwise if the table is compromised then any token ever generated can be decrypted. Further, unauthorized access to the detokenization service allows recovery of any USV from a token, and unlimited access to the tokenization service allows its misuse to create a rainbow table of all possible USV and tokens.

Figure 2.12 provides an overview of the tokenization environment. From a tokenization perspective, there are either authorized entities that include users and business applications that interface to the tokenization system or unauthorized entities that do not. Hence, the enterprise consists of a tokenization and a non-tokenization environments. Authorized entities are authenticated by the Tokenization Request Interface (TRI) for tokenization, detokenization, and possibly verification or other related reporting services. Communications between

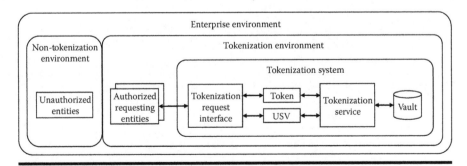

Figure 2.12   Tokenization environment.

the TRI and authorized requesting entities should also be secured; for details, see Chapters 4 and 5. The tokenization service might include a token vault but only interacts with a valid TRI and only responds to legitimate requests.

Regardless of the methods offered by the tokenization service, although it is more likely only a single method is supported, unlimited access to tokenization allows its misuse to create a dictionary table of all possible USV and tokens. Likewise, unauthorized access to detokenization (or verification) allows recovery of any USV from a token. Thus, the tokenization environment should be kept isolated from other services and unauthorized entities.

Chapter 3

Cryptographic Keys

This chapter builds on the information from previous chapters and provides further details regarding symmetric keys, asymmetric key pairs, and public key certificates. The information presented here remains largely algorithm agnostic, but some algorithm specifics are referenced where needed. And although some public key infrastructure (PKI) components are discussed here, this chapter does not address operational aspects; see *Security without Obscurity: A Guide to PKI Operations* [5].

- Chapter 1 provided a cryptography lexicon with a math refresher, commonly used notation, and conventional cryptographic terminology.
- Chapter 2 provided an overview of symmetric and asymmetric cryptography including encryption, hashes, integrity and authentication, non-repudiation, and tokenization.

The key management methods discussed in this chapter are used in various protocols which are addressed in Chapters 4 and 5. The key management schemes discussed in this chapter address both data in transition between a sender and a receiver, and data in storage such as a database environment. While key management schemes are introduced in this chapter, the key management lifecycle and cryptographic modules are discussed in Chapter 7.

3.1 Symmetric Keys

This section discusses various symmetric-based cryptographic schemes to establish symmetric keys, versus the next section which discusses asymmetric-based

33

cryptographic schemes to establish symmetric keys. Key establishment schemes include the following:

- Initial key
- Fixed key
- Master/Session key
- Derived unique key per transaction (DUKPT)

Key delivery schemes discussed in this section include the following:

- Faux key
- PKCS tokens
- Database encryption key management (DBEKM)

As discussed in Chapter 2 the same symmetric key is used for encryption versus decryption, for message authentication code (MAC) or keyed hash message authentication code (HMAC) to generate or verify an integrity check value (ICV), or for some tokenization methods. When a sender and receiver is involved, the same key must be shared by both entities. However, establishing the initial key (IK) is problematic. Without a key encryption key (KEK) to protect other keys, the IK needs to be securely exchanged in some manner. Historically, this has been accomplished using key components; see Figure 3.1. The term key component is defined in X9.24-1 standard [30].

> **Key Component**: one of at least two parameters having the format of a cryptographic key that is exclusive-ORed/ added modulo-2 with one or more like parameters to form a cryptographic key. A component is equal in length to the resulting key [30].

Note that exclusive OR (same as exclusive-ORed) is also defined in Chapter 1, and Annex: XOR Quick Reference provided a complete list of XOR values in hex and binary. Figure 3.1 shows an example of two entities, a sender and a receiver, exchanging key components to establish a symmetric key. In this scenario, the sender generates a 128-bit symmetric key and creates two 128-bit key components, sends both

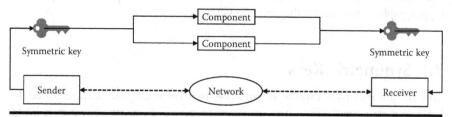

Figure 3.1   Symmetric IK.

components securely to the receiver, and the receiver recombines the components to install the symmetric key. The actual procedures will vary depending on the capabilities and expertise of the two participants with several viable options.

- The sender generates two random numbers as key components, assigns each component to separate holders, then each component holder hand delivers their components to two separate component owners at the receiver. Alternatively, the sender holders might separately send the components via letter post to the receiver holders.
- The sender generates a random key, a random number as the first key component, and XOR the key with the component to derive the second component. The sender then assigns each component to separate holders, who then securely transfer each component to separate receiver holders via hand delivery, letter post, or possibly secure email.

Alternatively (not shown in Figure 3.1), the sender generates a random number as the first component, and the receiver generates a random number as the second component. The sender assigns a component holder who securely transfers the first component to a specific receiver holder. Similarly, the receiver assigns a holder who securely transfers the second component to another sender holder. Both sides then combine their original and the delivered components to reconstitute the symmetric key.

Other key component procedures are possible. However, once the components have been exchanged and the symmetric key has been established, the components can then be reused for backup and recovery. Figure 3.2 shows an example of symmetric key recovery. The sender can retain the key components in a secure storage facility and maintain the component holders' responsibilities in the event that the key needs recovery due to some technical glitch. Likewise, the receiver can retain the key components in a secure storage facility and maintain the component holders' responsibilities in the event that the key needs recovery. In this manner, the components do not need to be reexchanged unless a new key is being redistributed. X9.24-1 provides requirements and recommendations for handling key components [30].

Once the symmetric key has been established, there are two basic operating methods: either fixed key or master key (MK)/session key (SK). Figure 3.3 shows

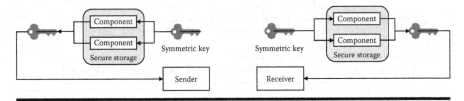

Figure 3.2   Symmetric key recovery.

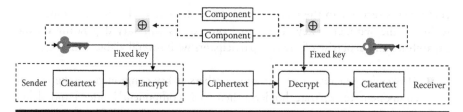

Figure 3.3   Symmetric fixed key.

an example of the fixed key method using key components to establish an initial symmetric key. The IK is used by the sender to encrypt cleartext and used by the receiver to decrypt ciphertext. Once the fixed key has reached the end of its life-cycle, it is replaced by exchanging new components all over again. Thus, once the IK has been established using key components with manual procedures, it remains "fixed" until it is replaced using the same manual procedures. X9.24-1 provides requirements and recommendations for the fixed key method [30].

Some systems might reuse the current fixed key to exchange a new key; how-ever, this violates a basic key management principle: keys are generated and used for an intended purpose. The fixed key lifecycle is intended to protect data by not overusing the encryption key. Repurposing the data encryption key (DEK) as a KEK at the end of the key lifecycle increases risk of a key compromise to the new key and consequently to the data.

Figure 3.4 shows an example of the MK/SK method using key components to establish an initial symmetric key. The IK is used as an MK to exchange one or more SKs. The sender encrypts a random SK using the MK and sends the ciphertext to the receiver who decrypts the ciphertext to recover the SK. Once the SK has been established, the sender encrypts cleartext using the SK and the receiver decrypts ciphertext using the SK. X9.24-1 provides requirements and recommendations for the MK/SK method [30].

When the SK has reached the end of its lifecycle, it is replaced by exchanging another SK using the MK. When the MK has reached the end of its lifecycle, it is

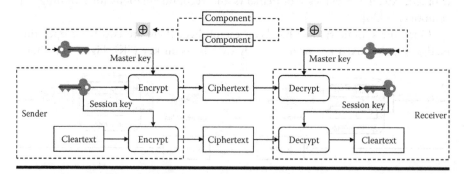

Figure 3.4   Symmetric MK/SK.

replaced by exchanging new components all over again. An alternative to redoing components is to exchange a new MK using the current MK; however, this is only valid if the current MK is not compromised. The MK is a KEK used to exchange the DEK so reusing it to exchange another KEK preserves its intended purpose and is compatible with the basic key management principle: keys are generated and used for an intended purpose.

Unfortunately, both fixed key and MK/SK share a common problem. Industry standards [30] require that any key used by a communicating pair be unique (other than by chance). This means that a host processing system communicating with hundreds, thousands, or even million terminal devices needs to manage a separate key per terminal. Using fixed key or MK/SK methods would necessitate a database of keys. Alternatively, the DUKPT (pronounced "duck putt") allows a host to manage many terminals with unique keys using a single base derivation key (BDK). X9.24-1 provides requirements and recommendations for the DUKPT method [30].

DUKPT is a key management scheme between a host system and many terminals although it can be used in many other scenarios.

- Figure 3.5 shows how a host uses the base derivation key (BDK) to generate and inject an IK into a terminal.
- Figure 3.6 shows how a terminal uses the IK to generate derived keys (DKs) to send encrypted transactions to a host.
- Figure 3.7 shows how a host receives and processes the encrypted transactions from a terminal having only the base derivation key (BDK).

Figure 3.5 shows how the host injects a unique IK into a terminal. The host encrypts a terminal identifier (TID) to generate an IK that is electronically injected into a terminal. The TID is unique to each terminal; consequently, each IK is unique to each terminal. The key injection is typically performed within a key injection facility (KIF) specifically designed and managed for key loading. A KIF has physical security, logical access controls, and monitoring. Once terminals are loaded with unique TID and IK, they are added to an inventory system and eventually shipped to their designated locations for physical installation.

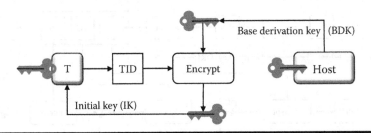

Figure 3.5   DUKPT IK.

Figure 3.6 shows how a terminal uses the IK to generate DKs per transaction to encrypt personal identification numbers (PINs). The terminal uses the transaction counter (TC) and the IK exactly once to generate the first DK. The IK is destroyed so it no longer resides within the terminal. If the terminal is compromised only an unused DK remains in the terminal. When a user enters a PIN, the DK is used to encrypt the PIN creating an encrypted PIN (EP). The EP, the TC, and the TID are sent to the host which only has the BDK. The terminal increments TC and uses the DK to generate the next DK. Again, if the terminal is compromised only an unused DK remains in the terminal. Each time a DK is used, the current EP, TC, and TID are sent to the host, and the TC is incremented to generate the next DK.

Figure 3.7 shows how the host processes a transaction received from a terminal having only the BDK. The transaction includes the EP, the TC, and the TID. First, the host uses the BDK to encrypt the TID for recreating the terminal's unique IK. Second, the host uses the IK with the TC to cycle through the derivation algorithm to determine the current DK. Third, the host uses the DK to decrypt the EP and recover the PIN. Once the PIN has been decrypted, the IK and the DK are erased and the host only retains the BDK. Note that the same DK might be inadvertently generated on different terminals at different times, but overall each DK is relatively unique to each terminal.

The DUKPT example discussed here is for securely transmitting a PIN from a terminal to a host.

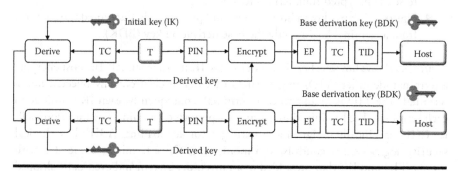

Figure 3.6 DUKPT terminal keys.

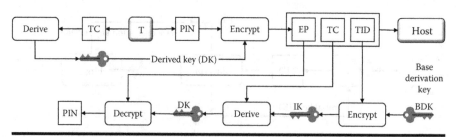

Figure 3.7 DUKPT host keys.

- The PIN is encrypted at the point of entry by the terminal
- The EP is transmitted from the terminal to the host
- The PIN is decrypted by the host for verification

The host might verify the PIN or possibly re-encrypted the PIN for further transmission to another network or host for verification. However, the DUKPT method can be used to establish an encryption key for any type of data or cryptographic function, not just PIN encryption. Any of these methods (fixed key, MK/SK, and DUKPT) can be used for establishing keys between communicating parties (e.g., sender and receiver).

Other methods can be used for delivering DEKs from a key management system to a data storage system, such as a database or other information repository. Some key delivery methods protect keys better than others, while others challenge basic cryptography industry practices. Figure 3.8 illustrates one method called faux key showing a database on the left communicating over a secure channel (TLS) to a key manager on the right. Transport Security Layer (TLS) is addressed in Chapter 5. This method is called faux key because the database spoofs the key manager by encrypting and decrypting a special data element that is used as a DEK. Cryptographic hardware security modules versus software modules are discussed in Chapter 7.

The database performs key initialization at start-up when it generates a DEK in system memory using some random number generation method. The database uses the cleartext DEK in memory to encrypt and decrypt local data. The cleartext key is sent to the key manager over a secure connection (TLS). The key manager, functionally unaware that the data encryption request is actually for a cryptographic key, dutifully encrypts the DEK and returns it to the database. The database stores the encrypted DEK on disk for subsequent restarts. When the system or database is restarted, the database sends the encrypted key is sent to the key manager for

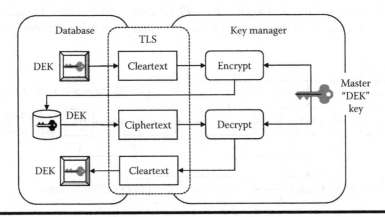

Figure 3.8   Faux key delivery.

decryption. Again, the key manager unaware that the data decryption request is for a cryptographic key, obediently decrypts the DEK and returns it to the database. The database uses the cleartext DEK in memory to encrypt and decrypt local data.

The key manager uses what is commonly called a "master" key to encrypt and decrypt the DEK, and often the MK is assumed to be a KEK. However, the DEK is actually a data element and not a cryptographic key the "master" key is actually another DEK and not a KEK. This difference is important when addressing key management controls as cryptographic modules are designed to protect keys and not disclose cryptographic material outside its cryptographic boundary. The key management lifecycle is discussed in Chapter 7. The faux key method is proprietary and is not defined in any industry standard or specification.

Figure 3.9 shows another key delivery method called PKCS token. The token is created by encrypting a DEK using a DK which is generated using a password-based key derivation function (PBKDF). The underlying function is HMAC using a hash algorithm (e.g., SHA-1 or SHA-2) as discussed in Chapter 2. The HMAC is repeated some number of times based on an iteration count. The initial HMAC inputs a password and a salt. The salt is a non-secret value used to deter rainbow table attacks by increasing the workload and making the DK relatively unique. Each subsequent HMAC inputs the result from the previous HMAC and reuses the password per the iteration count. The iteration count is based on the processing capacity and relative risks. Larger iteration counts increase workload to decrease risk, while smaller iteration counts increase risk. PBKDF is defined in PKCS#5 [33] which recommends a minimum of 1,000 iterations, whereas the NIST Special Publication 800-132 [39] recommends for critical keys or powerful systems upwards of 10 million iterations.

Figure 3.10 shows key delivery for the PKCS token method. The key manager uses the password and salt to generate the DK which is used to encrypt a randomly generated DEK to create the PKCS token. The password, salt, and PKCS token are sent from the key manager to the database which are stored to disk. The database uses the password (and salt) to unlock the PKCS token which allows the recovered DEK to be installed in memory for subsequent data encryption and decryption.

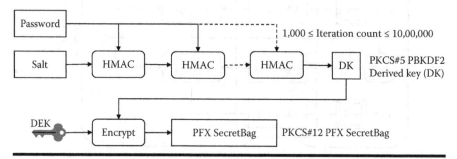

Figure 3.9   PKCS token PBKDF.

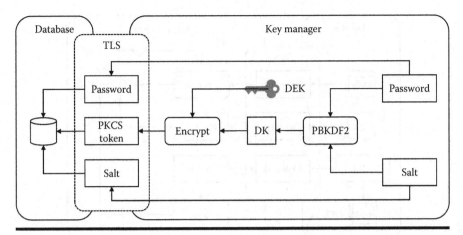

Figure 3.10   PKCS token delivery.

However, storing all three components (password, salt, and PKCS token) locally is basically equivalent to storing a cleartext DEK since all information needed to access the DEK is available. Alternatively, the key manager might provide only the PKCS token or password on-demand such that the database need not store both locally. Another option is to have a database administrator manually enter the password during database start-up. The PKCS token is defined in PKCS#12 [38].

Figure 3.11 shows the setup for another key delivery method called DBEKM. The key manager generates two keys: an actual MK that is KEK and an HMAC key (HK). The HK is encrypted using the MK and sent to the database. The HK is then erased so the key manager only retains the MK. The database stores the benign encrypted HK to disk and generates an identifier (ID) that is relatively unique to the database. The ID is likewise benign and might refer to a region, datacenter, server, or specific to a database volume, file, or column.

Figure 3.12 shows the key delivery for the DBEKM method. The database sends the encrypted HK and cleartext ID to the key manager over a secure

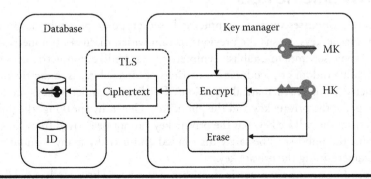

Figure 3.11   DBEKM setup.

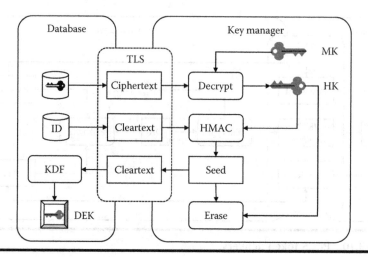

Figure 3.12 DBEKM key delivery.

communication. The key manager decrypts the HK using the MK, then uses the HK and ID as inputs to HMAC to generate a seed value. The seed is returned to the database and then the HK and seed are erased so the key manager only retains the MK. The database uses the seed as input into a KDF to generate a DEK in system memory. Note that the key manager does not contain the KDF and so cannot generate the DEK. The key manager does not violate its cryptographic boundary and protects keys at all times. Further, the database server only has benign data stored on disk and only uses key in system memory.

This section discussed several symmetric-based key establish schemes and key delivery schemes, and the next section discusses asymmetric-based cryptographic schemes.

3.2 Asymmetric Keys

This section discusses various asymmetric-based cryptographic schemes to establish symmetric keys, versus the previous section which discusses symmetric-based cryptographic schemes to establish symmetric keys. Unlike symmetric keys which are basically random or pseudorandom strings of binary bits, asymmetric keys are constructed using mathematical equations. Further, asymmetric keys are always built in pairs, the private key and the public key. Generally speaking, the public is derived from the private key, but the private key cannot be derived from the public key. Thus, the public can be safely distributed and used by many without risk to anyone determining the private key.

Depending on the asymmetric algorithm, asymmetric keys can be used for data integrity and authenticity, data confidentiality, or key management.

A. For data integrity and authenticity, the private key might be used to generate a digital signature, and the corresponding public key can be used to verify the digital signature. Asymmetric algorithms used for digital signatures can be reversible or irreversible.

B. For data confidentiality, the public key might be used for data encryption, and the corresponding private key can be used for data decryption. However, for encryption and decryption to be possible, the asymmetric algorithm must be reversible.

C. For key management, the public key might be used for key encryption, and the corresponding private key can be used for key decryption. When a symmetric key is encrypted using the public key at one location and decrypted using the private key at another location, this is called asymmetric key transport. However, for encryption and decryption to be possible, the asymmetric algorithm must be reversible.

D. For key management, the public and private keys might be used with another set of asymmetric keys to mathematically calculate a shared secret which can then be used to derive a shared symmetric key. When two parties exchange public keys and use them with their own asymmetric keys to calculate a shared secret, this is called asymmetric key agreement; the symmetric is not physically sent between the two parties. Asymmetric algorithms used for key establishment can be reversible or irreversible.

Cryptographic methods for data integrity and authentication (A) and data confidentiality (B) were discussed in Chapter 2. This section addresses key establishment, a general term for key transport (C) and key agreement (D) methods. Various asymmetric cryptographic schemes are used to establish symmetric keys which in turn are used to protect data. Figure 3.13 illustrates key transport using the Rivest–Shamir–Adleman (RSA) algorithm [9] defined in X9.44 [42]. The sender (Alice) uses the receiver's public key to encrypt an SK which only the receiver (Bob) can decrypt. The transport of the encrypted symmetric key from the sender to the receiver establishes the SK between the two parties. The RSA algorithm is reversible so keys can be encrypted and decrypted but irreversible algorithms cannot be used for key transport.

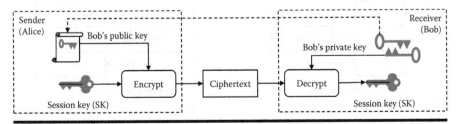

Figure 3.13   RSA key transport.

There are several alternatives for key transport. For example, the sender might encrypt a random number and transmit it to the receiver to be used as an SK. As another example, the sender might encrypt a random number and transmit it to the receiver as an ingredient to create a symmetric key. Another example is the sender might encrypt a random number and transmit it to the receiver to be used as an MK which in turn is used to exchange an SK. Each of these alternatives are valid key transport methods.

Note that the sender is shown using a public key (digital) certificate versus using a "naked" public key. Thus, the sender (Alice) uses the receiver's (Bob) digital certificate which contains Bob's public key. Digital certificates were introduced in Chapter 2 when addressing non-repudiation and are discussed in more details in the latter sections of this chapter. See also the Annex: X.509 Certificate Quick Reference for certificate formats.

Figure 3.14 demonstrates key agreement using the Diffie–Hellman (DH) algorithm [40] as defined in X9.42 [41]. For key agreement to work mathematically the first step is for both parties, the sender (Alice) and the receiver (Bob), exchange public keys as digital certificates. The second step, ignoring the underlying algebra, is each party computes the same shared secret using its asymmetric key pair and the other party's public key.

- Alice uses her public asymmetric key, her private asymmetric key, and Bob's public key.
- Bob uses his public asymmetric key, her private asymmetric key, and Alice's public key.

The third step is each party derives a symmetric key from the shared secret using a common KDF. The KDF allows Alice and Bob to derive the same symmetric

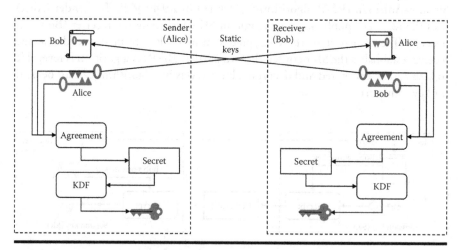

Figure 3.14   DH or ECDH key agreement.

key from the shared secret. The length of the symmetric keys is determined by the intended symmetric algorithm and its options, for example the Advanced Encryption Standard (AES) supports 128-bit, 192-bit, and 256-bit keys, whereas the length of the shared secret differs depending on the DH domain parameters and the length of the DH keys, so the KDF allows the key size to be derived from the shared secret.

Figure 3.14 also represents the Elliptic Curve Diffie–Hellman (ECDH) algorithm defined in X9.83 [43] which is an elliptic curve analogue of the DH key agreement mechanism defined in X9.42 [41]. Thus, the asymmetric keys used for DH key agreement might be DH keys or ECDH keys and interestingly the digital certificate encapsulating the public key is signed using a completely different algorithm (e.g., RSA or ECDSA).

SKs established using key transport or key agreement schemes are vulnerable if the asymmetric private keys are ever compromised. For example, an adversary who gains access to the private keys and has recordings of the network traffic can reestablish the SKs and decrypt the data hours, days, months, or even years later. Figure 3.15 shows the cryptographic countermeasure to this susceptibility called "forward secrecy" using ephemeral keys.

Ephemeral keys are by definition short-lived as opposed to long-term static keys. Both Alice and Bob have long-term keys consisting of a private key and a digital certificate. In addition, one (or both) has ephemeral keys consisting of a private key and a public key. For the purposes of this discussion, the underlying assumption is both have ephemeral keys. The ephemeral public key is not encapsulated within a certificate because the ephemeral keys' lifetime is only a few seconds or less. The ephemeral keys are generated, the public key(s) are exchanged, and the ephemeral keys are included as part of the second step to compute the shared secret.

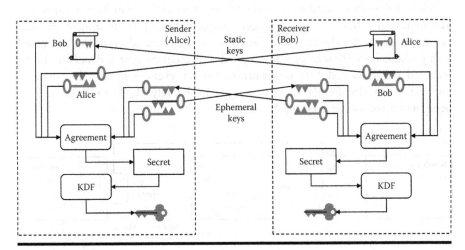

Figure 3.15   Ephemeral key agreement.

- Alice computes her shared secret using Bob's static and ephemeral public keys, and her own asymmetric static ephemeral key pair. Immediately after the SKs are generated, Alice destroys all the ephemeral keys.
- Bob computes his shared secret using Alice's static and ephemeral public keys, and his own asymmetric static ephemeral key pair. Immediately after the SKs are generated, Bob destroys all the ephemeral keys.

Once the ephemeral keys are erased an adversary cannot determine the SKs because the ephemeral private keys no longer exist. This presumes that the systems generating the ephemeral keys have not been compromised during their brief lifetime. Hence, forward secrecy is preserved. However, there are monitoring systems that rely on access to the server asymmetric keys which ephemeral keys interfere. Figure 3.16 illustrates how server static keys are replicated so monitoring system can duplicate the key establishment process. Arguably, monitoring systems are legitimate due to business and operational necessities; however, some security traditionalists will disagree. Businesses need to analyze customer interactions and operations need to troubleshoot network problems. Depending on network architectures and network components (e.g., routers, firewalls, load balancers) circumstances will vary.

The server asymmetric public and private static keys are replicated to the monitoring system typically using a manual process. A data tap captures all of the network traffic; every data packet is duplicated, including the key establishment packets and the subsequent encrypted data packets. The data packets are organized by a session ID and recorded to disk. The monitoring system has access to any certificates or public keys sent from clients to servers, and with access to the server static keys, can repeat the key establishment process which yields the SKs. The encrypted data packets can then be decrypted.

However, with forward secrecy, the server ephemeral private keys are missing. The monitoring systems can no longer complete the key establishment process, can no longer access the SKs, and therefore can no longer decrypt the encrypted data packets. Forward secrecy was designed to prevent encrypted data from being recorded and decrypted if the server private key was ever compromised. Ironically, forward secrecy also disables monitoring systems that rely wholly on the server keys being replicated for key reestablishment.

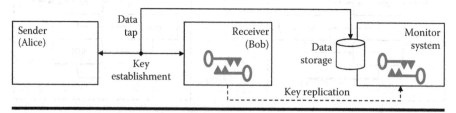

Figure 3.16 Key establishment monitoring.

3.3 Certificates and PKI

Certificates and PKI were introduced in Chapter 2 when discussing non-repudiation. There are various types of PKI credentials such as OpenPGP [44] message formats, PKCS#8 [35] for private key information, and PKCS#12 [38] for personal information exchange including private or public keys. This book focuses on X.509 certificates which only include public keys. Digital certificates defined in X.509 standards [45,46] and [47] contain five major components:

1. a public key,
2. the public key owner's information,
3. the public and private key pair information,
4. the certification authority's (CA) information, and
5. the CA digital signature over the previous four components.

See the Annex: X.509 Certificate Quick Reference for details. The public key is mathematically related to its private key so the digital certificate represents information about the key pair and the keys' owner. Most importantly, the certificate signature (5) provides a cryptographic binding between the public key (1) and the owner information (2). The binding is essentially an attestation by the CA that the key pair belongs to the owner. Additionally, the CA signature also cryptographically binds the CA information (4) and the key pair information (3) to the owner information (2) and public key (1). Figure 3.17 correlates additional certificate details to the certificate chain for a common PKI hierarchy.

The subject-related information includes its primary name, public key and related algorithm identification, the key usage indicators, and any subject alternate names (SANs). The key usage might be explicitly requested by the subject in the

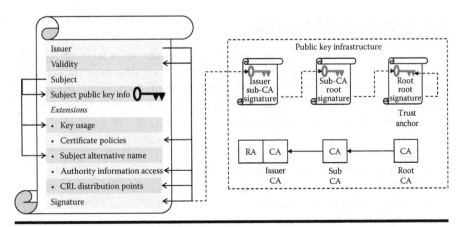

Figure 3.17   Certificates and PKI.

certificate signature request (CSR) submitted to the registration authority (RA) or implicit based on the RA or CA selected by the subject. Any alternate names might be explicitly requested in the CSR or provided to the RA using an out-of-band channel.

The issuer-related information includes its name, its certificate policy and practices, and certificate status accessibility such as a certificate revocation list (CRL) location or an online certificate status protocol (OCSP) responder.

The issuer-provided information includes the subject's public key validity dates and the CA signature on the certificate. The certificate's validity dates are based on the CA policy and certificate practices statement. The certificate signature is generated by the CA using its secured asymmetric private key and verified using the CA's public key. The CA public key is encapsulated in the issuer CA certificate. Each certificate's signature is verified using the public key in the next certificate within the certificate chain.

- The subject certificate's signature is verified using the issuer CA certificate.
- The issuer CA certificate's signature is verified using the subordinate CA certificate.
- The subordinate CA certificate's signature is verified using the root CA certificate.
- The root CA certificate's signature is verified using its own public key.

Some PKI might not employ an intermediate (subordinate) CA or might have more than one intermediary CA, so the length of the certificate chain may vary. The recipient of the subject's certificate is called the relying party because it must trust the RA and CA. However, the relying party needs to validate the complete certificate chain, called certificate validation.

3.4 Certificate Validation

Certificate validation is a complex process that includes verification of multiple X.509 data fields for multiple certificates. The first step is to determine the complete certificate chain from the end user certificate to the root CA certificate, such that if any certificate is missing the validation fails, and processing stops. Otherwise, for each certificate, check the following items.

1. Verify the certificate name
2. Verify the certificate validity period
3. Verify the algorithm and key usage
4. Verify the certificate signature
5. Verify the certificate status
6. Verify the critical extensions

If any item fails for any of the certificates, the validation fails and processing stops. Otherwise, if all of the items for all of the certificates verify, then and only then the subject public key can be used per the key usage declarations. However, above and beyond certificate validation, the relying application might have additional restrictions. For example, specific end user certificates or CA certificates might be required based on a white list. As another example, a specific X.509 extension might be required for processing. If any of the required certificate information is missing or invalid, the application might likewise stop processing. Verification details are discussed as follows.

1. Verify the certificate name.
   - The subject certificate name matches the subject name.
   - The issuer CA certificate name matches the issuer CA name.
   - The intermediate CA certificate name matches the intermediate CA name.
   - The root CA certificate matches the root (trust anchor) CA name.

   If the names do not match the validation fails. For example, browsers are known for name mismatch errors when the uniform resource locator does not match the server common name, but many browsers allow the user to accept an invalid certificate anyway. For example, a user might enter www.one.example.com, but the certificate subject name might differ such as www.example.com or some other name.

   However, certificates have two identity fields: the basic Subject field and the SAN extension. The SAN might contain other identities such as www.one.example.com and www.two.example.com so any match verifies the name. However, a single name mismatch for any of the certificates in the chain fails the certificate validation.

2. Verify the certificate validity period.

   If the current date and time is not between the certificate not-before and not-after dates and times, the certificate is invalid. The validity dates for each certificate must be legitimate otherwise the chain fails the certificate validation. Expired certificates should not be used as the validity periods are risk based correlating the public key with the private key's cryptoperiod.

3. Verify the key usage.

   If the certificate presented is not compatible with the intended cryptography functions, the public key should not be misused. For example, key management keys should not be used for digital signatures, DEKs should not be used for key management, and digital signature keys should not be used for data encryption or key management.

   Key usage is defined in two extensions: key usage and extended key usage. The former extension indicates the cryptographic functions such as digital signature, key transport or key agreement, or data encryption. The latter extension identifies the application purpose such as server authentication, client authentication, or code signing. The first extension is a fully defined bit map so there is no room left for other indicators. The second extension uses object identifiers (OIDs) so it is infinitely extensible.

4. Verify the certificate signature.
Each certificate's signature is verified using the public key in the next certificate within the certificate chain. The subject certificate is verified using the issuer CA certificate, the issuer CA certificate is verified using the next level CA certificate such as an intermediate CA certificate, and the final intermediate CA certificate is verified using the root CA certificate. The root CA certificate is self-signed and used to verify itself; however, it is preinstalled in a trust store.

Any certificate signature that fails to verify invalids the certificate chain so the subject certificate cannot be used. Failure might occur from constructing the chain incorrectly or possibly one of the certificates has been altered. Regardless, an invalid chain is a void subject certificate.

5. Verify the certificate status.
The subject certificate should contain access information to a status service. The CRL Distribution Points extension refers to a CRL. Alternatively, the Authority Information Access extension might provide location to an OCSP responder. However, the CRL download might fail or the OCSP might not respond, or the CRL or OCSP signatures might not verify.

If the certificate status cannot be verified then either its validity must be assumed with an appropriate risk or the subject certificate must be rejected. Depending on the business risks and application environment the relative risks need to be evaluated. For example, if the subject certificate status cannot be verified at one point it might be verified at a later time. But if the verification is for a real-time transaction then its status is critical.

6. Verify the critical extensions.
X.509 extensions are tagged using OIDs and marked as either critical or non-critical. If any extension is marked critical but the verification process does not recognize the OID then the certificate validation fails and the subject certificate is invalid. Extensions marked non-critical can be ignored if unrecognized but otherwise should be processed.

In addition to certificate validation, the Digital Signature Guideline (DSG) [14] and the PKI Assurance Guideline (PAG) [15] acknowledge that operational and legal controls need to be in place for genuine non-repudiation services. Operational controls consist of each PKI participant (subject, RA, CA, relying party) performing according to an agreed-upon set of rules to establish trust. Legal controls include two primary areas: dispute resolution and chain of evidence.

Chapter 4

Authentication Protocols

This chapter discusses various authentication protocols (procedures to provide data integrity and authenticity) versus encryption protocols (procedures to provide data confidentiality) discussed in Chapter 5. While this chapter does not (and cannot) address every authentication protocol, framework, method, or algorithm, it does provide a decent overview that the reader can use as reference material and as a foundation for performing security assessments. Some authentication protocols include encryption but are primarily used for authentication and not confidentiality.

Authentication is distinguishable from authorization. Authentication is the set of security controls to verify an entity and potentially grant access to system resources including data and applications. Authorization is the set of security controls to validate permissions for accessing system or network resources.

4.1 Domain Name System Security (DNSSEC)

The Domain Name System (DNS) is a set of distributed databases that contain various types of resource records (RRs) for managing Internet domain names. Basically, DNS translates domain names like www.example.com to an Internet Protocol (IP) address (198.51.100.0). DNS also provides reverse lookups; an IP address is translated to the corresponding domain name. The right-most name (e.g., .com) is known as the top-level domain (TLD) name. Other TLD include .com for commercial entities, .org primarily for nonprofit organizations, .edu for higher education institutions, .gov for US government agencies, .mil for US military forces, and two-letter country codes based on ISO 3166-1 [48] such as .au for Australia, .jp

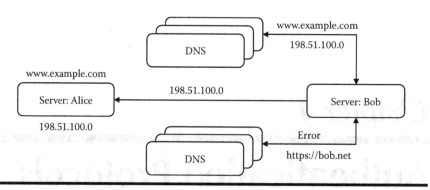

Figure 4.1   DNS example.

for Japan, .ru for Russian Federation, and .us for United States. ISO also offers an Online Browsing Platform*.

The second-level domain name (e.g., www.example.com) is separated from the TLD by a period, with an unlimited number of lower levels (e.g., third level, fourth level) likewise separated by periods. The prefix www denotes a World Wide Web server, whereas ftp is a file transfer protocol server and mail is for an email server. The Internet Corporation for Assigned Names and Numbers† manages the TLD and many other unique identifiers. Figure 4.1 gives a two simplistic DNS examples: a successful lookup and a failure. For the first example, the server Bob connects to the server Alice using the name www.example.com. Bob submits the name to a DNS server which may communicate to other DNS services, and the translated IPv4 address 198.51.100.0 is returned to Bob allowing a connection to Alice. For the second example, Bob gets an error for the name bob.net so without an IP address the connection fails.

However, if any of the DNS RRs are counterfeit, Alice might connect to the wrong server (not Bob) but be unaware of the dishonest connection. There are three basic DNS protocol attacks [50]. DNS cache poisoning is where the wrong record information is injected onto a DNS server. DNS spoofing is when an illegitimate server intercepts a valid DNS request and returns an invalid DNS response. DNS ID hacking is when an illegitimate server masquerades as a legitimate DNS server and provides inaccurate RRs. Domain Name System Security (DNSSEC) is an authentication scheme designed to mitigate these types of DNS attacks.

Figure 4.2 provides an overview of DNSSEC cryptography. DNSSEC uses Public Key cryptography to sign and authentication RRs but does not use Public Key infrastructure (PKI) or digital certificates. See Chapter 2 for digital signatures and Chapter 3 for digital certificates and PKI considerations. Rather, the Public

---

* www.iso.org/obp/ui/#home
† www.icann.org/

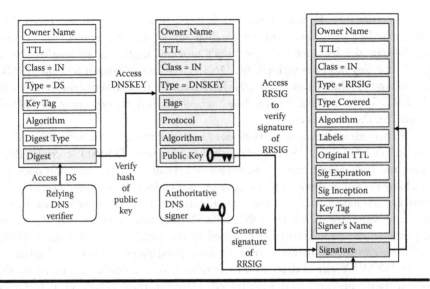

Figure 4.2   DNSSEC cryptography.

Keys are stored in DNSKEY RRs, and the corresponding private keys are stored by the authoritative DNS signers. The digital signatures are stored in RRSIG RRs. The digest (hash) of the DNSKEY RRs is stored in DS RRs. Further, DNSSEC does not provide confidentiality.

- The Domain Name System Key (DNSKEY) RR includes Owner Name, Algorithm identifier, and the Public Key value. The Public Key is Base64 encoded. RFC 4034 [49] mandates Rivest–Shamir–Adleman (RSA) digital signatures with Secure Hash Algorithm (SHA-1) hash and includes the Digital Signature Algorithm (DSA) with SHA-1, but the Message Digest 5 (MD5) hash is no longer recommended.
- The Resource Records Signature (RRSIG) RR includes Owner Name, Algorithm identifier, a Labels field to help resolve the key Owner Name, Signature Expiration and Signature Inception validity dates with a ±68-year limit, a Key Tag which provides a mechanism for selecting a Public Key efficiently, the Signer's Name, and the Signature over various RRSIG fields.
- The DS RR includes Owner Name, a Key Tag, Algorithm identifier, a Digest (hash) identifier, and a Digest of the DNSKEY RR.

The requesting server (e.g., Bob) is essentially a relying DNS verifier to verify the hash (Digest) of the Public Key which is then used to verify the signature. The DS record is accessed to find the DNSKEY record, and the Digest (hash) in the DS record is used to verify the Public Key in the DNSKEY record. In lieu of a PKI and digital certificates, the hash of the Public Key is stored in a separate record than the Public Key itself, thus arguably the dual records are akin to separate accounting ledgers, the legitimacy of one ledger provides legitimacy of another. Next, the Public Key has been verified, the DNSKEY record is used to find the RRSIG record, and the Public Key in the DNSKEY record is used to verify the signature in the RRSIG record. Once the signature has been verified, the content of the RRSIG record can then be trusted.

The requesting server (e.g., Bob) does not have the target server's (e.g., Alice) Public Key until the DNS responds with the appropriate DNSSEC records. Thus, Alice and Bob do not need to establish any keys directly. Further, Bob does not need any keys of her own. And, because DNSSEC does not use digital certificates, Bob does not have a certificate chain to validate, but does need to verify each Public Key and signature within the DNS RRs. The legitimacy of the RRSIG record depends on the digital signature provided by the authoritative DNS signer (Bob) and the controls Bob maintains over the corresponding private key. The legitimacy of the DNSKEY record depends on the validity of the Public Key based on the Digest (hash) provided in the DS record. However, there is no central authority (e.g., PKI) vouching for the trustworthiness of the DS records. See Figure 4.3 for a cryptographic architecture perspective of DNSSEC and the corresponding DNS records.

Alice is the asymmetric key owner. She provides to DNS her public in a DNSKEY record, the hash of her Public Key in a DS record, and a digital signature using her private key in a RRSIG record. Bob is the relying party (RP). He retrieves the records from DNS, verifies Alice Public Key in the DNSKEY record using the hash in the DS record, verifies Alice's digital signature in the RRSIG record using her Public Key, and consequently verifies the RRSIG content based on the signature verification. Bob can then access Alice's Internet site using the DNS records protected by Alice's hash, Public Key, and digital signature.

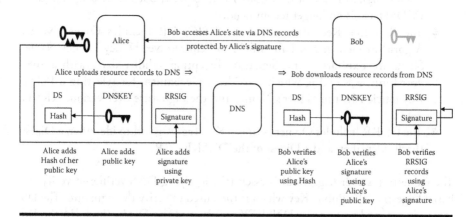

Figure 4.3 DNS cryptographic architecture.

4.2 Domain Keys Identified Mail (DKIM)

Domain Keys Identified Mail (DKIM) is an authentication scheme that enables validation of email messages from one organization to another using digital signatures. The signer might be the individual email sender, the sender's desktop agent, the organization email system, or an intermediary email transfer system. Further, the verifier might be the individual email receiver, the receiver's desktop agent, the organization email system, or an intermediary transfer email system. According to RFC 6376 [51], the reputation of the signer is the basis for evaluating whether to trust the email message. See Figure 4.4 for a cryptographic architecture perspective of DKIM and the associated DNS records.

Alice sends an email to Bob. The signer adds the DKIM header to the message which contains the digital signature, reference to an DNS RR, a list of which message elements were hashed for the signature, and other related DKIM information. In this example, Header 2 and the Body text were hashed for the signature; thus Header 1 and Header 3 have not been signed. The DNS record contains the signer's Public Key such that the verifier can use the Public Key to verify the digital signature in the DKIM header. The signer generates the digital signature using the corresponding private key.

A common DKIM implementation is for the signer and verifier to be an organization email system. Alice sends the email from her workstation and her organization email system signs the message. Bob's organization email system verifies the signature and delivers Alice's message to Bob's workstation. Neither Alice nor Bob needs cryptographic keys. Alice's organizational email system manages a private key and provides its corresponding Public Key in a DNS RR. Bob's organizational email system does not manage cryptography keys, rather Alice's Public Key is obtained from the DNS record referenced in the DKIM header.

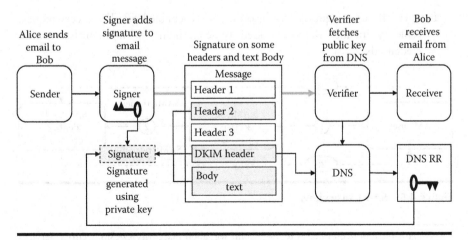

Figure 4.4   DKIM cryptographic architecture.

4.3 Security Assertion Markup Language (SAML)

Security Assertion Markup Language (SAML) is an authentication and authorization scheme developed by the Organization for the Advancement of Structured Information Standards (OASIS) Security Services* Technical Committee [52]. The scheme also supports confidentiality. SAML is an Extensible Markup Language (XML)-based [53] framework for communicating authentication, entitlement, and attribute information. Figure 4.5 provides a high-level overview of SAML. There are many logical entities within the SAML framework but for the purposes of this book only three are introduced: the SAML user, the SAML-enabled service provider (SP), and the SAML identity provider (IdP). The SAML framework supports many scenarios which can be described by the message path.

One scenario is a simple user access to an SAML-enabled SP where the SP gets the SAML token from the IdP, path = (1, 2, 2, 1).

Path (1) the user requests access to an SAML-enabled SP. The access request typically incudes the user's identity (e.g., name) and authentication credentials (e.g., password, digital signature, mobile device information).

Path (2) the SP sends an SAML request to the SAML IdP. The SAML request includes the user identity and authentication requests.

Path (2) the SAML IdP returns an SAML response (also called the SAML token) to the SP. The SAML response includes the user authentication validation information and authorization attributes.

Path (1) the SP allows (or denies) user access based on the authentication validation information and authorization attributes in the SAML token.

A similar scenario is user access to an SAML-enabled SP where the SP redirects the user to the IdP to get an SAML token, path = (1, 2a, 2b, 1).

Path (1) the user requests access to an SAML-enabled SP. The access request typically incudes the user's identity (e.g., name) without authentication credentials.

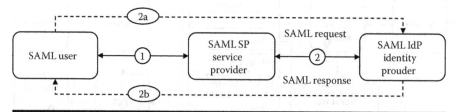

Figure 4.5 SAML overview.

---

* www.oasis-open.org/committees/tc_home.php?wg_abbrev=security OASIS Security Services (SAML) Technical Committee

Path (2a) the SAML-enabled SP redirects the user request as an SAML request to the SAML IdP. The SAML request only includes the user identity such that the IdP engages the user to provide authentication credentials (e.g., password, digital signature, mobile device information).

Path (2b) the SAML IdP returns an SAML response (token) to the user. The SAML token includes the user authentication validation information and authorization attributes.

Path (1) the SP allows (or denies) user access based on the authentication validation information and authorization attributes in the SAML token.

Another scenario is when a user gets the SAML token from the IdP before accessing the SAML-enabled SP, path = (2a, 2b, 1, 1).

Path (2a) the user sends an SAML request to the SAML IdP. The SAML request includes the user's identity (e.g., name) and authentication credentials (e.g., password, digital signature, mobile device information).

Path (2b) the SAML IdP returns an SAML response (token) to the user. The SAML token includes the user authentication validation information and authorization attributes.

Path (1) the user requests access to an SAML-enabled SP using the SAML token.

Path (1) the SP allows (or denies) user access based on the authentication validation information and authorization attributes in the SAML token.

For the last scenario, the SP and the IdP might be the same organization where an SAML token is issued to a user for subsequent access. Each SAML token has a time to live (TTL) such that an expired token is invalid. Thus, the user would need to periodically refresh its SAML token. The SAML token is basically used as an access ticket.

There are many other possible paths that correlate to the mapping of the SAML request–response message exchanges onto standard communication protocols which are called SAML *protocol bindings* (or just *bindings*) such as Simple Object Access Protocol and Hypertext Transfer Protocol (HTTP). Regardless, SAML messages are expected to be exchanged over a Secure Socket Layer (SSL) or Transport Layer Security (TLS) connection. See Chapter 5 for a discussion of SSL and TLS.

Figure 4.6 shows an SAML cryptographic architecture for sending request or response messages between an SAML server (SP or IdP) and an RP (user or SP) depending on the scenario, over an SSL or TLS connection. The SAML assertions (authentication or authorization information) are digitally signed by the asserting party (AP) (IdP) within the SAML message (request or response). The SAML messages are digitally signed by the sender (IdP, SP, or user). Within the SSL/TLS session, the SAML messages are also encrypted and have an keyed hash message authentication code (HMAC) for integrity. The SSL/TLS session keys (one for

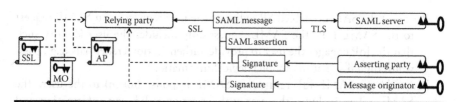

Figure 4.6   SAML cryptographic architecture.

encryption, another for HMAC) are established using an asymmetric key management scheme. See Chapter 2 for details on encryption or HMAC and Chapter 3 for details on key establishment schemes.

The SAML assertion signature is generated by the AP so that entity manages a private key and provides its certificate to the RP. The SAML message signature is generated by the message originator (sender) so that entity manages a private key and provides its certificate to the RP. The SSL/TLS connection is offered by the SAML server so that entity manages a private key and provides its certificate to the RP (SSL/TLS client). Thus, for authentication and authorization, the RP might only have Public Keys relative to the various certificates. If mutual TLS authentication is used, then the RP would also have a certificate and a private key. However, it was mentioned that SAML also supports confidentiality as shown in Figure 4.7 for various SAML messages.

Any SAML message might include encrypted data using the Encrypted ID option. Likewise, authentication assertions or authorization attributes might also be encrypted using the Encrypted Assertion or Encrypted Attribute options. All three encrypted options include the Encrypted Data and Encrypted Key fields. Instead of defining its own key management scheme, the SAML Encrypted Key field uses the XML Encryption scheme [54]. The XML Encryption scheme includes an Encryption Method field used to define the cryptographic algorithms, a Key Info field used to define the key establishment method, and a Cipher Data field. Depending on the key establishment method, the sender and receiver will have additional keys (see Figure 4.8).

For example, the SAML message in Figure 4.8 includes an Encrypted ID with the Encrypted Key using a Diffie–Hellman (DH) key establishment scheme in the

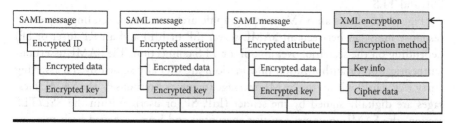

Figure 4.7   SAML confidentiality.

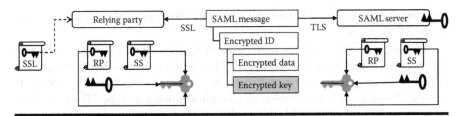

Figure 4.8   SAML cryptographic architecture.

XML Key Info field. In addition to the SSL private key, the SAML server (SS) has another certificate with a private key and a copy of the RP certificate. Similarly, in addition to the SSL certificate, the RP has another certificate with a private key and a copy of the SS certificate. The SAML server uses the two DH certificates and its DH private key to compute a shared secret and derive a symmetric key for the Encrypted Data. Likewise, the RP uses the two DH certificates and its DH private key to compute the same shared secret and derive the same symmetric key for the Encrypted Data.

4.4 Open Authorization (OAUTH)

Open Authorization[*] (OAUTH) is an open standard to enable authorization (not necessarily authentication) for web, mobile, and desktop applications. More specifically, OAuth 2.0 authorization framework[†] enables a third-party application to obtain limited access to an HTTP service. OAUTH should not be confused with the Initiative for Open Authentication[‡] (OATH) framework. Figure 4.9 shows the basic OAUTH protocol [55] which includes servers (client, service, authorization,

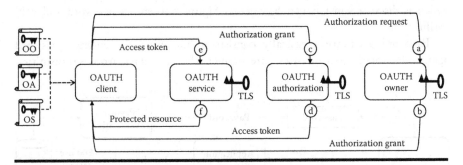

Figure 4.9   OAUTH cryptographic architecture.

---

[*] https://oauth.net/
[†] https://oauth.net/2/
[‡] https://openauthentication.org/

and owner) and messages (authorization request, authorization grant, access token, protected resources).

The message flow is initiated by (a) authorization request and (b) authorization response messages between the OAUTH client and the OAUTH owner. The OAUTH owner grants (or denies) the client access to the requested service. If granted, the message flow continues by (c) authorization grant and (d) access token messages between the OAUTH client and the OAUTH authorization (OA) service. The OA service (which might be the same entity as the OAUTH owner) provides an access token. The message flow is completed by (e) access token and (f) protected resource messages between the OAUTH client and the OAUTH service (OS). The access token enables the OAUTH client to acquire the OS's resources.

OAUTH is expected to run over the most current TLS. Thus, each server will provide its Public Key certificate with the OATH client and manage its corresponding private key. The OAUTH owner (OO) server sends its certificate to the OAUTH client to establish the first TLS session, the OA server sends its certificate to the OAUTH client to establish a separate TLS session, and the OS sends its certificate to the OAUTH client to establish another TLS session. Thus, the OAUTH client might only have Public Keys relative to the various certificates. If mutual TLS authentication is used, then the RP would also have a certificate and a private key.

4.5 Password and PIN Verification

Knowledge factor authentication is the "something you know" method which includes passwords and personal identification numbers (PIN). The methods for transporting passwords versus PIN are very different, as are the methods for verifying passwords versus PIN. Passwords and PIN are encrypted during transportation, which is discussed in Chapter 5, whereas Figure 4.10 shows password and PIN verification.

Password verification basically consists of matching the entered password against the stored password in a secure manner. The entered password is transmitted

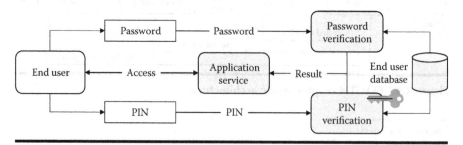

Figure 4.10   Password and PIN verification.

securely (discussed in Chapter 5) from the end-user process to the password verification process. The password verification process fetches the stored password from the end-user database which might contain hundreds, thousands, or millions of passwords. Thus, the verification process needs an end-user identifier to locate the correct end-user profile in order to fetch the correct password. The passwords are also stored in a secure manner. Likely, the stored password versus the transmitted password formats are different; the verification process needs to convert the formats into a common format in order to compare the two passwords. The comparison result (match or no match) is provided to the application service. The application service makes the final decision to grant or deny access as it might be using other authentication services in addition to password verification, or supports alternative authentication methods such as challenge questions.

Password storage methods rarely keep cleartext passwords; unauthorized access to the end-user database would compromise all passwords. Further, an administrator with authorized access might be coerced to reveal the passwords, so it is better to avoid storing cleartext passwords altogether. Stored passwords might be encrypted using a cryptographic key, but since password verification is typically done using only software, protecting keys is problematic. Thus, most password storage is done using a hash algorithm. However, as discussed, hash algorithms are susceptible to dictionary attacks, commonly called rainbow tables. All possible passwords can be hashed such that an attack who has access to the end-user database can simply look up the hash against the rainbow table to determine the password.

Password hashing uses two additional mechanisms to deter dictionary attacks: password salting and iteration counts [39]. As shown in Figure 4.11, password salting adds a random value to the password before hashing such that the resulting hash value is changed by the addition of the salt. The salt is not intended to be kept secret; secret salting is analogously called peppering. Rather, the salt increases the work factor for creating the rainbow tables. Consider a work factor for one 8-character password allowing uppercase and lowercase letters, numerical digits, and special characters.

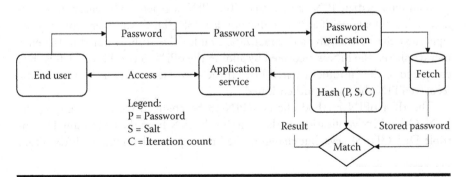

Figure 4.11   Password verification.

- Password alphabet: 26 lower + 26 upper + 10 digits + 8 special = 70 possible characters
- Possible 8-character passwords: 70^8 or about 576 trillion possible passwords

Thus, a rainbow table for no-salt (or pepper) with one iteration would have half-a-quadrillion entries. But, modern computers have clocked modern hash algorithms (e.g., SHA-512) at a million or more per second so the 576 trillion hash calculations using a thousand computers could be computed in about two months. Given the availability of cloud computing, the attack is feasible and the costs are realistic. Adding a random salt to each password replicates the work factor for each password, so an end-user database with a thousand passwords would increase the overall work from two months to 166 years. Of course increasing the computer power reduces the time factor, but the attacker is not interested in cracking all the passwords, just an administrator's password. So if the attacker knows which end-user profile is an administrator, the work factor is pragmatically reduced to a single password.

Password iteration count is the number of times the hash is applied to the password (and salt) for storage. Iterations counts merely increase the work factor, but can delay password verification, affecting the end-user experience. NIST recommends a minimum of one thousand iterations, but for more powerful servers an iteration count of 10 million may be appropriate [39] when computing password-based key derivation functions. Irrespective of the salt and iterations, the password verification process needs to obtain the transmitted password as cleartext to apply the hashing so that it can be compared to the stored hashed password.

PIN verification for payment cards is very different than password verification. The PIN is a 4- to 12-digit number defined in ISO 9564 [56] and associated to the card's primary account number (PAN). The PAN is a 12- to 19-digit number defined in ISO/IEC 7812 [57]. Unlike passwords, the PIN might be bank issued or customer selected. Bank-issued PIN might be derived directly from the PAN or a random number, similar to a customer-selected PIN.

As shown in Figure 4.12, the IBM 3624 PIN verification* is based on a PIN offset (oPIN). The oPIN is generated by subtracting the customer-selected PIN from an intermediate PIN value (iPIN). The iPIN is generated by encrypting validation data (vData) with a PIN verification key (3K-3DES) and then replacing the ciphertext characters using a decimalization table. The oPIN is stored in the end-user database. The PIN is recovered by adding the oPIN to the iPIN which is then compared to the customer-entered PIN. If the customer-entered PIN matches the recovered PIN the user is authenticated.

The IBM oPIN method allows a PIN to be changed without changing the PAN. Other PIN verification methods derive the PIN from the PAN using DES or triple-DES (3DES) keys, but changing the PIN requires changing the PAN. From

---

* z/OS Cryptographic Services ICSF Application Programmer's Guide www.ibm.com/support/knowledgecenter/en/SSLTBW_2.1.0/com.ibm.zos.v2r1.csfb400/csfb4za2597.htm

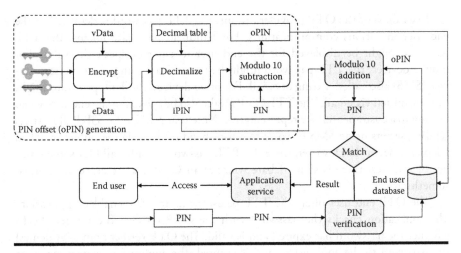

Figure 4.12   IBM 3624 PIN verification.

a cryptographic architecture viewpoint, password verification schemes typically use a keyless hash; however, PIN verification methods use DES or 3DES cryptographic keys. Newer PIN verification schemes using AES are in development; draft X9.132 [58].

4.6 One-Time Password (OTP)

One-time passwords (OTPs) are short-lived authentication credential which are not to be confused with the cryptographic method one-time pad (OTP). Cryptographic OTP is a key management method for using a different encryption key for each message. Authentication OTP uses passwords with a limited TTL denoted by the clock icon. Figure 4.13 depicts an OTP architecture showing a client-based end user, an application, a verifier, and a provider. The OTP provider might be a host-based server sending a TTL password to a client-based end user. The end user might employ a workstation, laptop, tablet, or mobile device. Alternatively, the OTP provider might be client-based software running on the end-user device or a separate hardware token held by the end user.

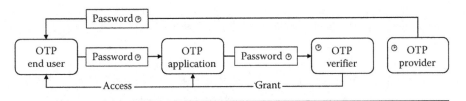

Figure 4.13   OTP cryptographic architecture.

Regardless of the OTP provider origins, the TTL password is delivered to the end user in various communications. For handheld hardware tokens, the TTL password might be displayed for the end user to enter or speak the value. For mobile devices, the TTL password might be transmitted using short message service (SMS) also called texting or email. For other devices, the TTL password might be transmitted via email. The TTL OTP might also be spoken to the end user when talking to a customer service representative. Note that NIST 800-63B [59] restricts sending secrets using SMS or voice to out-of-band devices via the public switched telephone network. However, since the TTL password is only valid for some number of minutes, there is some debate whether an OTP is a secret, semisecret, or something less.

The OTP end user offers the TTL password to an OTP-enabled application. The application checks the password with the OTP verifier. The verifier checks whether the password has expired and is valid. The OTP verifier grants (or denies) the password to the application, and if granted, the application enables access to the end user. OTPs are typically random values to be unpredictable without using cryptographic keys, but a critical component are accurate clocks for the OTP provider and OTP verifier to maintain the TTL expiration.

Chapter 5

Encryption Protocols

This chapter discusses various encryption protocols (procedures to provide data confidentiality) versus authentication protocols (procedures to provide data integrity and authenticity) discussed in Chapter 4. While this chapter does not (and cannot) address every encryption protocol, framework, method, or algorithm, it does provide a decent overview that the reader can use as reference material and as a foundation for performing security assessments. Some encryption protocols include integrity and authentication mechanisms but are primarily used for data confidentiality and not authentication.

5.1 Transport Layer Security (TLS)

Transport Layer Security (TLS) is the successor to Secure Socket Layer (SSL); both protocols provide secure communication over a computer network. It is a common misnomer to say SSL but mean TLS and often the term SSL/TLS is used. Many implementations include both protocols, but they are not interoperable; however, earlier versions of TLS supported backwards compatible with SSL. Further, SSL has been deprecated due to a variety of vulnerabilities.

- SSL v1.0 was developed by Taher Elgamal* while he worked at the Netscape Corporation but it was never release publically.
- SSL v2.0 was released in February 1995.
- SSL v3.0 was released in November 1996 and later codified as a historical document Request For Comment (RFC) 6101 [60] in August 2011.
- TLS v1.0 based on SSL v3.0 was published as RFC 2246 [61] in January 1999.

---

* Father of SSL: https://en.wikipedia.org/wiki/Taher_Elgamal

- TLS v1.1 was published as RFC 4346 [62] in April 2006.
- TLS v1.2 was published as RFC 5246 [63] in August 2008.
- TLS v1.3 has been in development since April 2014.

The various TLS v1.3 drafts make protocol changes to v1.2 including mandating ephemeral keys for forward secrecy and deprecating Rivest–Shamir–Adleman (RSA) since it cannot support ephemeral keys. Ephemeral keys were discussed in Chapter 3. TLS v1.2 consists of two layers: the TLS handshake protocol and the TLS record protocol. The TLS handshake exchanges static X.509 [45] certificates to establish a shared secret from which two keys are derived: the encryption key and the Hash Message Authentication Code (HMAC) key. Figure 5.1 shows a dotted line between the Transport Layer Security (TLS) client and TLS server representing the transport keys. The session keys (SKs) (encryption and HMAC) might be established using key transport (e.g., RSA) or key agreement (e.g., Diffie–Hellman [DH]); and key agreement might use ephemeral keys for forward secrecy.

Once the TLS handshake protocol has established the SKs, the TLS record protocol encrypts each message between the SSL client and the SSL server. The TLS Ciphertext record shows four elements: the Content Type, the Protocol Version, the Length field, and the Generic Cipher field. The Generic Cipher field includes an HMAC of the cleartext data and the encrypted data. There are three encryption options for the Generic Cipher: stream cipher encryption, block cipher encryption, and the authenticated encryption with additional data encryption. The TLS handshake protocol negotiates the cipher suite that defines the key establishment scheme for the SK, the cipher option, the encryption algorithm, and the hash algorithm for the HMAC. From a cryptographic architecture perspective, the TLS protocol has the following keys:

- The TLS client has its public and private transport keys, the SSL server X.509 certificate, and the two derived SKs: the encryption key and the HMAC key.
- The TLS server has its public and private transport keys, the SSL client X.509 certificate, and the two derived SKs: the encryption key and the HMAC key.

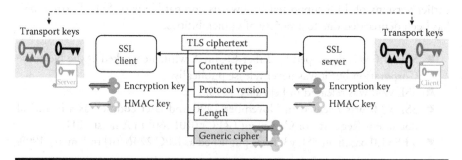

Figure 5.1   TLS cryptographic architecture.

Some key establishment schemes such as RSA key transport do not require client transport keys, only server transport keys are necessary. The TLS client encrypts a random number using the TLS server keys which both entities use to derive the SKs. If ephemeral keys are used, then in addition to the static TLS client and host transport keys, one or both entities would have another asymmetric key pair and share the public key (PK) with the other entity. Ephemeral PKs are not encapsulated in X.509 certificates due to the key pair brief lifecycle, typically a few milliseconds. However, as mentioned, RSA cannot support ephemeral keys.

5.2 Internet Protocol Security (IPsec)

Internet Protocol Security (IPsec) [64] is an encryption and authentication protocol for the Internet Protocol (IPv4 and IPv5) data packets. IPsec offers two independent security mechanisms: the Encapsulating Security Payload (ESP) [66] provides data packet confidentiality and optionally integrity, and the Authentication Header (AH) [65] provides data packet integrity and authenticity. AH is not an authentication protocol; it does not authenticate an individual, application, system, or device; rather it provides protection of the data packet within the IPsec protocol. Figure 5.2 shows how the AH is created and used with IP headers.

The AH is first inserted between the IP header(s) and the Transport Control Protocol (TCP) header with the Integrity Check Value (ICV) set to null (binary zeroes), and then an HMAC using an HMAC key is computed over the following elements: the IP header(s), the AH (with ICV = 0), the TCP header, and the data payload. The ICV field is then updated with the HMAC value. The receiver recomputes the HMAC in a similar matter to verify the integrity of the IP packet, and arguably, if only the sender and receiver have the HMAC key then the receiver can authenticate the sender. Conversely, the ESP offers integrity with encryption; Figure 5.3 shows how the ESP is created and used with IP headers.

The ESP header is inserted between the IP header(s) and the TCP header, the ESP trailer is appended after the data payload, and if the ESP ICV is used it is further appended after the ESP trailer. An HMAC using an HMAC key is computed over the following elements: the ESP header, the cleartext TCP header, the cleartext data payload, and the cleartext ESP trailer. The ESP ICV is updated with

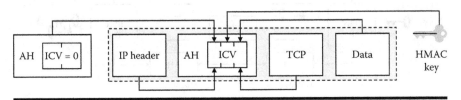

Figure 5.2   IPsec AH.

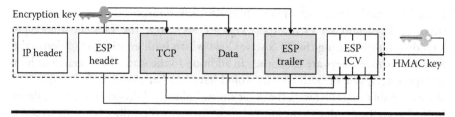

Figure 5.3   IPsec ESP.

the HMAC value. For confidentiality, the following elements are encrypted using an encryption key: the TCP header, the data payload, the ESP trailer. Regardless of whether ESP or AH or both are used, Figure 5.4 shows IPsec from a cryptographic architecture perspective.

For an IPsec connection between Alice and Bob, each party exchanges PKs (or preferably X.509 certificates. Thus, Alice has its public and private transport keys, and Bob's PK (or certificate), and Bob has its public and private transport keys, and Alice's PK (or certificate). The IPsec transport keys are used with the Internet Key Exchange protocol to establish two encryption keys and two HMAC keys. Alice uses the first SK pair (encryption, HMAC) to send IP packets to Bob, and Bob uses the second SK pair to send IP packets to Alice. Conversely, Alice uses the second SKs to receive IP packets from Bob, and likewise Bob uses the first SK pair to receive IP packets from Alice.

5.3 Secure Shell (SSH)

Secure Shell (SSH) is a protocol for remote login and other network services over an insecure network. The protocol is described in four parts: architecture per RFC 4251 [67], authentication per RFC 4252 [68], transport per RFC 4253 [69], and connection per RFC 4254 [70]. While SSH offers password- and signature-based authentication, it is primarily an encryption protocol to protect administrative

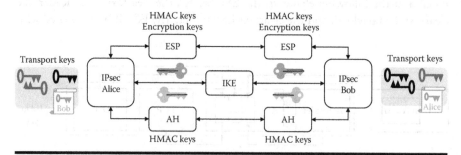

Figure 5.4   IPsec cryptographic architecture.

commands between an SSH client and SSH host. The transport protocol defines the encryption and key management, and the authentication protocol defines digital signatures. Figure 5.5 shows both the SSH cryptographic architecture.

Each SSH packet is composed of five elements: packet length, padding length, payload, padding, and HMAC. SSH integrity consists of an HMAC computed over the cleartext of the first four elements (packet length, padding length, payload, and padding). SSH encryption consists of encrypting the same four elements after the HMAC has been computed. The HMAC key and the encryption key are derived from a shared secret computed using the DH key agreement scheme. Thus, from a cryptographic architecture perspective, the SSH client and the SSH host have the following keys:

- For SSH transport, the SSH client has its DH public and private keys, the SSH host PK (preferably encapsulated within an X.509 certificate), and the two derived SKs: the encryption key and the HMAC key.
- For SSH authentication, the SSH client might also have its digital signature (e.g., RSA) private key.
- For SSH transport, the SSH host has its DH public and private keys, the SSH client PK (preferably encapsulated within an X.509 certificate), and the two derived SKs: the encryption key and the HMAC key.
- For SSH authentication, the SSH host might also have the client's digital signature PK (preferably encapsulated within an X.509 certificate).

If ephemeral keys are used, then in addition to the static SSH client and host DH public and private keys, one or both entities would have another DH key pair and share the PK with the other entity. Ephemeral PKs are not encapsulated in X.509 certificates due to the key pair brief lifecycle, typically a few milliseconds.

RSA key transport which does not support ephemeral keys was added to SSH transport RFC 4432 [71] later the same year. For RSA key transport, only the SSH host needs a key pair. The SSH client encrypts a random number using the

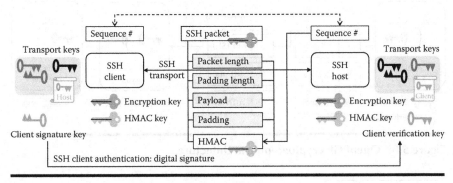

Figure 5.5   SSH cryptographic architecture.

SSH host PK, the SSH host decrypts the random number, and both sides derive the SKs (encryption and HMAC). In addition to the SSH host, the SSH client might also have its own RSA key pair to digitally sign a challenge so that the SSH host can authenticate the SSH client.

5.4 Pretty Good Privacy (OpenPGP)

OpenPGP [72] is a standardized security protocol based on Pretty Good Privacy® (PGP) originally developed by Philip R. Zimmermann[*] published in 1991. PGP® was a collection of software functions providing encryption, digital signatures, and key management. OpenPGP messages are composed of various packets identified by tag numbers. Figure 5.6 provides two examples of messages sent from Alice to Bob and Chuck, one message using asymmetric key encryption, and another using symmetric key encryption. Both messages use symmetric data encryption for confidentiality and hashing for data integrity.

From a cryptographic perspective, each participant has a key ring containing its public and private keys, and the PKs of the others. Any symmetric keys are encapsulated within the messages and not the participants' key rings.

- Alice's key ring: contains her private and public keys, Bob's PK, and Chuck's PK.
- Bob's key ring: contains his private and public keys, Alice's PK, and Chuck's PK.
- Chuck's key ring: contains his private and public keys, Alice's PK, and Bob's PK.

The first message (left) is composed of four packets: two Tag 1 packets, a Tag 9 packet, and a Tag 19 packet. The two Tag 1 packets are public-key encrypted

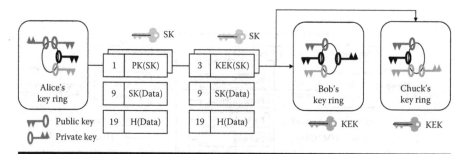

Figure 5.6 OpenPGP cryptographic architecture.

---

[*] http://philzimmermann.com/EN/background/index.html

session key packets. These packets contain an encrypted SK using the recipient's PK. The single Tag 9 packet is a symmetric-key encrypted session key packet. This packet contains data encrypted using a symmetric SK. The final Tag 19 packet is a modification detection code packet which contains a hash of the data.

- Bob can decrypt only one of the Tag 1 packets using his private key yielding the SK which is used to decrypt the Tag 9 packet which yields the data. Bob uses the Tag 19 packet is used to verify the integrity of the decrypted data.
- Chuck can decrypt only the other Tag 1 packets using his private key yielding the SK which is used to decrypt the Tag 9 packet which yields the data. Chuck uses the Tag 19 packet is used to verify the integrity of the decrypted data.

The second message (right) is likewise composed of four packets: two Tag 3 packets, a Tag 9 packet, and a Tag 19 packet. The two Tag 9 packets are symmetric-key encrypted session key packets. These packets contain an encrypted SK encrypted using a key encryption key (KEK). Each packet uses a different KEK generated using different passphrases that Alice has shared separately with Bob and Chuck. The single Tag 9 packet is a symmetric-key encrypted session key packet. This packet contains data encrypted using a symmetric SK. The final Tag 19 packet is a modification detection code packet which contains a hash of the data.

- Bob can decrypt only one of the Tag 1 packets using the passphrase provided by Alice, yielding the SK which is used to decrypt the Tag 9 packet which yields the data. Bob uses the Tag 19 packet is used to verify the integrity of the decrypted data.
- Chuck can decrypt only the other Tag 1 packets using the passphrase provided by Alice, yielding the SK which is used to decrypt the Tag 9 packet which yields the data. Chuck uses the Tag 19 packet is used to verify the integrity of the decrypted data.

OpenPGP can be used for sending messages or storing information. Other functions include digital signatures and data compression. Digital signatures are supported using Tag 2 Signature Packets. OpenPGP uses the term "certificate" but does not support X.509 certificates but rather employs various PK and private key packets that constitute the key ring.

5.5 Password and Personal Identification Number Encryption

Knowledge factor authentication is the "something you know" method which includes passwords and personal identification numbers (PIN). The methods for transporting passwords versus PIN are very different, as are the methods for verifying passwords versus PIN. Password and PIN verification was discussed in Chapter 4, whereas Figure 5.7 shows password versus PIN encryption. The upper part of the diagram shows an end user entering a password for password verification; the lower part of the diagram shows an end user entering a PIN for PIN verification. Regardless of the knowledge factor, the password (or PIN) needs to be transported from the point of entry to the point of verification. The end user identifier (e.g., name) is used by the verification process to fetch the end user profile from a database.

The password flow (upper diagram) consists of the end user entering and encrypting the password, transporting the encrypted password to the verification system, and the password decrypted for verification. Rarely are any cryptographic keys used exclusively to encrypt a password. Rather, if the password is encrypted at all, it is often within a TLS connection. Thus, from a cryptographic architecture perspective, the end user system has the PK (or preferably an X.509 certificate) of the verification system. The verification system has its public and private key pair. The encryption and HMAC SKs are negotiated during the TLS handshake, and the password is transported within the TLS data packet. The encrypted password is transported from the end user to the verification system.

The PIN flow (lower diagram) consists of the end user entering the PIN, but a dedicated process performs the PIN encryption. The encrypted PIN block is transported from one system to another, translated from one symmetric key to another. The number of PIN translation will vary as the encrypted PIN block traverses multiple networks until it reaches the PIN verification system. The PIN verification then decrypts the encrypted PIN block and verifies the PIN as described in Chapter 4. Figure 5.8 provides an example of PIN payment process.

The issuer provides a payment card and PIN to the cardholder using separate delivery methods, such as two different letters. The cardholder makes a purchase at a merchant submitting the payment card and entering the PIN into a point-of-sale (POS) terminal. The terminal encrypts the PIN using a symmetric PIN encryption key (PEK). The first PEK is shared with the acquirer system that provides payment services to the merchant. The acquirer translates the PIN from the PEK shared

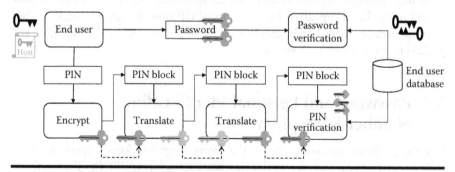

Figure 5.7   Password and PIN encryption.

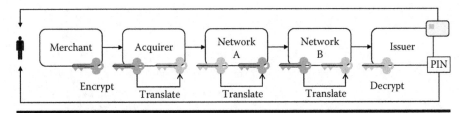

Figure 5.8   PIN payment process.

with the POS terminal to another PEK shared with network A that provides pay-ment services to the acquirer. Network A translates the PIN from the PEK shared with the acquirer to a different PEK shared with network B that provides payments services to the issuer. Network B translates the PIN from the PEK it shares with network A to the PEK it shares with the issuer. The issuer decrypts the PIN so it can verify the PIN using PIN verification keys.

Figure 5.8 PIN payment process.

Chapter 6

Architectures

Architectures define the various components and the interactions between those components that comprise the structure of a complete system. However, architectures can have more than one focus with distinct viewpoints. This chapter considers the similarities and differences between application architectures, network architectures, information architectures, and of course cryptographic architectures.

6.1 Application Architecture

Application architectures provide a graphical description of the implementation for the business logic which can be portrayed in a wide variety of methods. As discussed in Chapter 1, diagrams might be simple cartoons. Hopefully however, the security professional is provided with more informative architectural diagrams. Figure 6.1 continues the network scenario introduced in the first chapter. An organization provides web services to individuals and a business portal (BP) for external business applications (BAs). The backend application (App) and database (DB) servers support the web and BP servers located in the network demilitarized zone (DMZ).

Figure 6.1 provides an application process flow view. Requests are received by either the web servers or the BP servers and when authenticated, passed onto the App servers for processing. Customer profiles are fetched from the DB servers by the App servers. Some request processing will update the DB. Responses are returned from the App servers to the network request source, either the web servers or the BP servers, and then onto the original request source, either the external BA or individual browsers. From a security perspective, Figure 6.1 includes the following information:

■ Individuals connect to the web servers using Hypertext Transfer Protocol Secure (HTTPS) which is HTTP over Transport Layer Security (TLS).

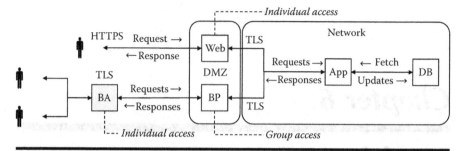

Figure 6.1   Application process flows.

- Individuals are authenticated and authorized by the web servers using identity-based authentication.
- Other individuals use a local BA that connects to the BP server over TLS.
- Other individuals are presumed to be authenticated and authorized by the BA servers, and connections are authenticated and authorized by the BP server using group-based authentication.
- The web server and the BP server both connect to the App server using TLS from the DMZ to the network.
- The App server connects to the DB server over an open connection within the network boundary.

However, from a cryptographic perspective, Figure 6.1 provides inadequate information.

- The TLS cipher suites defining key management algorithms, symmetric algorithms and key size for encryption, and hash algorithm for the HMAC are not specified.
- The TLS certificates defining the public key algorithms, key size, and hash algorithm for the digital signature are not specified.
- Hashing algorithms, salt size, and iteration counts for password hashing are not specified.
- Key management practices for any of the servers are not specified.

There are many other types of application architecture diagrams. For example, Figures 6.2 and 6.3 are sequence diagrams for the same scenario. Sequence diagrams are often used to provide additional messaging details. Figure 6.2 depicts web-based transactions, and Figure 6.3 shows portal-based transactions. As shown in Figure 6.2, requests flow from individuals using browsers to the web servers; the BA and BP servers are skipped. The first sequence illustrates the web server rejecting the request due to an authentication error; a response error is returned to the individual. The second sequence describes a successful

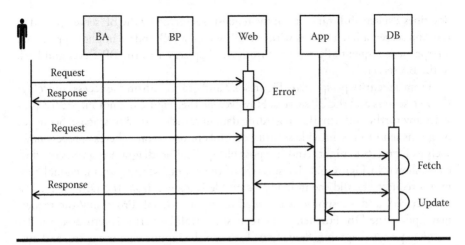

Figure 6.2   Application web sequence diagram.

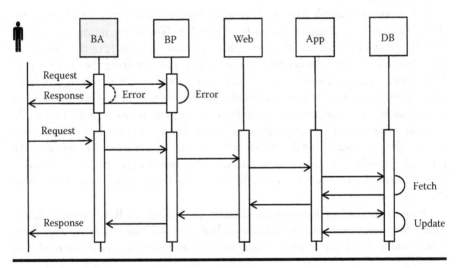

Figure 6.3   Application BP sequence diagram.

transaction: the request is received by the web server, passed to the App server, a fetch occurs with the DB server, a DB update might happen, and a response is sequentially returned from the App server to the web server and back to the end user browser.

As shown in Figure 6.3, requests flow from individuals using an external BA servers and onto the BP servers. The first sequence illustrates either the BA server or the BP server rejecting the request due to an authentication error. If the BA server rejects the request then the BP server never sees the message. If the BP server rejects the request then a response error is returned to the BA server. The second sequence describes a successful transaction: the request is received by the BP server, passed to the App server, a fetch occurs with the DB server, a DB update might happen, and a response is sequentially returned from the App server to the BP server and back to the BA server.

From a security perspective, Figures 6.2 and 6.3 reconfirm the access controls at the web servers and the BP servers. However, neither Figure 6.2 nor Figure 6.3 provides any further information regarding data in transit or data in storage. Sequence diagrams tend to not provide security controls information, whereas process flows such as Figure 6.1 might. Another possible application diagram is a classical flow chart shown in Figure 6.4. Irrespective of the various servers, an individual submits a request, if valid the individual's profile is fetched from the DB, the request is processed, and a response is returned to the individual. Processing the request may update the DB. Further, if the request is invalid an error is returned. Similar to the sequence diagrams, flow charts focus on the inputs, data processes, and outputs, but not so much on security controls. However, the validity check reconfirms access controls.

An alternate to application process flows, sequence diagrams, and flow charts is a state transition diagram shown in Figure 6.5. Notwithstanding the various servers, the system rests in idle state until a request changes it to the validation state. An error returns the system back to the idle state awaiting the next request. Otherwise, a fetch transitions the system to a data state for acquiring the individual's profile record. A successful fetch changes the system to a process state. A successful response returns the system from either process or data state to the idle state, or potentially an error returns the system from either data or process state to the idle state. State transition diagrams are not widely used but can identify processing conditions that other application diagrams might inadvertently overlook. Otherwise, they are not typically used to determine information security (IS) controls.

Another method to document application processing is a RACI matrix. RACI stands for responsible, accountable, consulted, and informed. The purpose for a RACI is to describe the various process roles. Roles can be a software or hardware

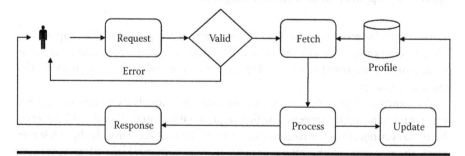

Figure 6.4   Application flow chart.

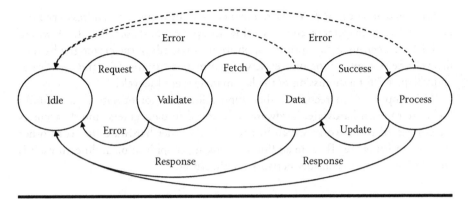

Figure 6.5   Application state transition diagram.

component, a manual process, a group, or even an individual. For this scenario, shown in Table 6.1, the roles are the individuals, and the various servers: the BA server, the BP server, the Web server, the App server, and the DB server. The roles are mapped to the messages: the request, the response, and errors.

- Request messages: the individual is responsible to initiate the request; the BA, BP, and Web servers are accountable to handle the request; the App server is responsible for processing the request; and the DB server is informed when updates are needed.
- Response messages: the individual is responsible for accepting the response; the BA, BP, and Web servers are accountable to handle the response; the App server is responsible for processing the response; and the DB server is informed when updates are needed.
- Error messages: the individual is consulted when an error occurs; the BA, BP, Web, and App servers are responsible for returning error messages; and the DB is informed when updates are needed.

RACI do not typically convey IS controls unless processes are purposely added to the matrix. However, a RACI is often built from other application plans so unless other diagrams have incorporated security controls, it is unlikely any would be

Table 6.1   Application RACI Chart

Process	Individual	BA	BP	Web	App	Database
Request	R	A	A	A	R	I
Response	R	A	A	A	R	I
Error	C	R	R	R	R	I

incorporated into the RACI chart. Further, it is infrequent to address cryptography or key management controls using an application-based RACI. However, RACI have been used to capture responsibilities regarding the cryptographic key lifecycle. See Chapter 3 for an overview of symmetric, asymmetric, and certificates and Chapter 7 for a discussion of the key management lifecycle.

It is important to recognize that applications do not operate in a vacuum. Software runs on hardware, hardware is deployed in datacenters, and datacenters are connected to networks which in turn rely on other hardware that runs other software or firmware. Thus, in addition to looking at application architectures, it is equally important to consider network architectures.

6.2 Network Architecture

Network architectures convey equipment, locations, and connectivity information. Equipment includes mainframes, various servers, and a variety of network appliances. Servers range from dedicated web servers, App servers, DB servers, file servers, and virtual servers running hypervisors that logically "slice" the hardware server into multiple instances. Network appliances include routers, firewalls (FWs), load balancers, switches, hubs, and other devices. Other appliances are functional specific such as DBs, log management systems, traffic monitoring system, and even cryptographic hardware security modules (HSMs). These latter appliances are sometimes treated as servers while other times are considered network devices; it often depends on the culture and experience of the network engineers. See Figure 6.6 for a network diagram of the ongoing scenario used throughout this book, organized into zones: the external Internet, the DMZ, and the internal network.

Figure 6.6 shows the usual servers in the DMZ: the web servers, the BP servers, and the remote access servers (RASs). The diagram also shows the other servers in the network zone: the App servers, the DB servers, the software server (SS), and the admin servers (ASs). In addition to the servers, the network diagram shows routers (R) located in the Internet zone, the DMZ, and the network zone. FWs separate the DMZ from the Internet and the network zone. All network traffic flow through the FWs where FW rules control which ports and protocols are permitted.

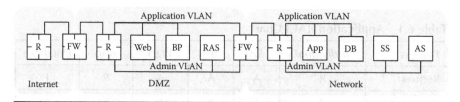

Figure 6.6   Network diagram.

Not shown or addressed are multiple FWs, web application firewalls (WAFs), application firewalls (AFs), or virtualization. Multiple FWs are commonly used to thwart hackers from using zero-day attacks, auto-script attacks, or lagging security configurations. For example, the FW shown between the Internet and the DMZ might be two different systems where the chance of the same vulnerability occurring on both FWs is very low. Auto-scripts designed to attack one system have a lesser chance of success against a different system. Further, a delayed patch on one system should have minimal effect on the other system.

WAFs and AFs interrogate network traffic beyond port and protocol FW rules. WAF or AF might run on traditional FWs, dedicated servers (not shown) or on the functional servers (e.g., Web, BP, or RAS). While WAFs and AFs are valid IS controls, they typically do not incorporate cryptography; thus they are not discussed further in this book.

Virtualization refers to hardware servers running hypervisors to enable resource sharing among multiple application instances running on the same hardware. Some virtualized servers can share resources among themselves across hardware platforms. Virtualization technology does not implement or rely on cryptography, rather applications running in virtual environments might employ cryptography; thus virtualization is not discussed further in this book.

Figure 6.6 also shows the various communication channels and virtual local area network (VLAN) connections. Inbound traffic from the Internet is directed by the external router to the external FW residing within the DMZ. The external FW filters messages and the DMZ router directs requests to either the web servers or the BP servers over the application VLAN, often called an "application rail" to collectively refer to other similar VLAN. Once the request is recognized by either server, the DMZ router redirects requests to the internal FW. The internal FW also filters messages and the network router sends requests to the App server over the "application rail" for processing. Further, the App server interfaces to the DB server over the same application rail via the network router.

Responses are returned by the network and DMZ routers over the network application rail from the App server to either the original Web or BP server through the internal FW. Once handled by the Web or BP servers the response is returned to the Internet via the DMZ and external routers over the DMZ application rail through the external FW. However, the network diagram does not address security controls for the application rail.

■ The HTTPS access to the Web server is not documented, and the TLS tunnel end point is not specified. The tunnel might terminate at the external FW in the DMZ, the router in the DMZ, or the Web server in the DMZ.
■ The TLS access to the BP server is not documented, and the TLS tunnel end point is not specified. The tunnel might terminate at the external FW in the DMZ, the router in the DMZ, or the Web server in the DMZ.

- The TLS connection from the Web server to the App server over the application rail is not documented, and the TLS tunnel end points are not specified. The tunnel might begin at the Web server or the internal FW and terminate at the App server or some intermediate network device such as a load balancer.
- The TLS connection from the BP server to the App server over the application rail is not documented, and the TLS tunnel end points are not specified. The tunnel might begin at the Web server or the internal FW and terminate at the App server or some intermediate network device such as a load balancer.

In addition to handling request and response messages, Figure 6.6 also depicts the "admin rail" in the DMZ and network zones. Administrators use the AS to manage the SS for pushing software patches to the other servers. The AS is also used by administrators to configure the other servers. Admins can access the AS internally when connected to the network zone, or externally using the RAS.

Administrators connect to the RAS via the Internet router, through the external FW, and via the DMZ router. Once authenticated and authorized, admins connect to the AS via the DMZ router, through the internal FW, and via the network router. Regardless, whether admins connect externally or internally, the AS authenticates and authorizes admins. Access to servers (App, DB, SS) within the network zone is via the network router. Connections to servers (Web, DP, RAS) within the DMZ are via the network router, through the internal FW, and via the DMZ router. The network diagram only provides connection information for a single datacenter, and further does not address security controls for the admin rail.

- The virtual private network (VPN) access to the RAS is not documented, and the TLS tunnel end point is not specified. The tunnel might terminate at the external FW in the DMZ, the router in the DMZ, or the RAS in the DMZ.
- The TLS connection between the RAS and the AS is not documented, and the TLS tunnel end points are not specified. The tunnel might begin at the RAS or the internal FW and terminate at the AS or some other intermediate network device such as a load balancer.
- The secure shell (SSH) transport connections and authentication methods between the AS and all other servers in the DMZ and network zone are not documented.
- The code integrity mechanisms provided by the SS and validated by all other servers in the DMZ and network zone are not documented.

Figure 6.7 addresses connectivity between datacenters and backup sites. For this scenario, there are two datacenters, the Region West and the Region East. The two external routers outside the DMZ are cross-connected over the Internet such that if a request arrives at one datacenter, but the local network connection is unavailable, the request is routed to the other datacenter. The two network zones are similarly cross-connected but over dedicated telecommunication lines to keep the App

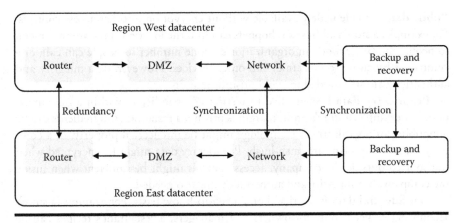

Figure 6.7   Datacenter diagram.

servers and DB servers synchronized. Each network zone has another dedicated line to external backup and recovery (BR) sites. Each datacenter has its own offsite BR services but are also cross-connected over dedicated telecommunication lines to keep the backup information synchronized. However, the datacenter diagram only provides connection information and does not address security controls.

- The IPsec connection between the two external routers is undocumented.
- The IPsec connection between the two network zone routers is undocumented.
- The IPsec connections between the datacenters and the BR sites are undocumented.
- The IPsec connection between the two BR sites is undocumented.

Clearly the IS controls documented by the various application diagrams need to be reflected in the network diagrams. Further, the information technology and the IS controls need to align and be represented in the network diagrams. These tasks are typically addressed by documentation, interviews, and analysis as discussed in Chapter 8. However, the end goal is to produce a cryptographic architecture.

6.3 Information Architecture

Information architectures identifies what data is stored or processed, where the data is stored or processed. Many organizations employ a data classification scheme with corresponding security requirements. For example, a data classification simple scheme might have three levels from lowest to highest security levels.

1. Public data
2. Proprietary data
3. Confidential data

Public data is made widely available without encryption or other access controls. For example, a store's address so shoppers can find the location, a restaurant's menu so people can order food, an organization's phone number so people can call, or a company's brochure so consumer can order services. However, data integrity and authenticity are still needed to avoid misinformation.

Proprietary data is controlled to restrict accessibility to within an organization. For example, a store's profit margin is private, a restaurant's ingredients can be nonpublic, an organization's technology might be intellectual property, or a company's marketing plans are hush-hush. Proprietary data might be encrypted when transported outside the company, access controls might be sufficient when inside the company, but integrity and authenticity are also needed.

Confidential data is restricted on a need-to-know basis. For example, a store's accounting ledger is only for owners and managers, a restaurant's recipes can be secret, an organization's acquisition is covert, or a company's undisclosed stock dividend is kept quiet. Confidential data might be encrypted anywhere it is stored, but integrity and authenticity are also needed.

However, such a minimal classification model might be too simplistic. For example, identification data such as account numbers, employee identification numbers, or customer numbers are a special type of confidential data. As another example, authentication data such as personal identification numbers (PINs) or passwords that grant access to networks, systems, or applications are another exceptional type of confidential data. Cryptographic data such as symmetric keys or asymmetric private keys are not the same as PINs or passwords, as they require much stronger controls than lesser data. Consequently, the first book [4] in this series offered a six-level data classification example, from lowest to highest security level.

1. Public data
2. Proprietary data
3. Confidential data
4. Identification data
5. Authentication data
6. Cryptographic data

Each data classification has its own corresponding security requirements. An organization's data classification policy, standards, and practices should clearly articulate its data protection security requirements. Thus, knowing where data is located and its corresponding classification helps defines the security controls based on the associated security requirements. See Figure 6.8 for an example of information diagram showing numerous data elements located on routers, FWs, and the various web, BP, RAS, App, DB, SS, and AS servers.

Network information includes Internet Protocol (IP) addresses, FW rules, ports, and protocol numbers. Routers use IP addresses to manage traffic among

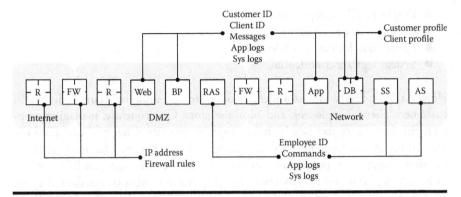

Figure 6.8   Information diagram.

the numerous network devices and various servers. FWs use IP addresses and rules to permit or block traffic based on the allowed ports and protocols. FWs or web servers might run WAFs that perform a deeper analysis of the data packet content.

- Port and protocol numbers are public data.
- IP addresses are considered proprietary data.
- FW rules are categorized as confidential data.

Application information includes customer identification (ID), client ID, messages, application (App) logs, system (sys) logs, customer profiles, and client profiles. Web servers use the customer ID to forward legitimate messages to the App servers but block illegitimate or expired customer ID. BP servers use the business client ID to forward legitimate messages to the App servers but block illegitimate or expired client ID. The App servers use the customer ID or client ID to fetch the corresponding customer profile or client profile from the DB servers to process the messages.

- Customer ID is proprietary.
- Client ID is proprietary.
- Messages are proprietary.
- Application logs are confidential.
- System logs are confidential.
- Customer profiles are confidential.
- Client profiles are confidential.

Administrative information includes employee ID, commands, application logs, and system logs. The RAS uses the employee ID to forward valid commands to the ASs but blocks invalid commands. The AS uses the employee ID to forward related commands to the SS.

- Employee ID is proprietary.
- Commands are confidential.
- Application logs are confidential.
- System logs are confidential.

However, proprietary and confidential data are accessible by many individuals: customers, clients, employees, and administrators. Consequently, managing cryptographic keys as regular data is an unacceptable practice. Chapter 3 discussed the importance of managing keys securely using various schemes. Chapter 7 discusses the significance of cryptographic modules and the key management lifecycle. An extremely important security axiom is that cryptographic keys are not data, they are used to protect data, and therefore cannot be managed as data. Thus, in addition to application architectures, network architectures, and information architectures, there is an essential need for cryptographic architectures. The lack of cryptographic architectures is a clear and present risk.

6.4 Cryptographic Architecture

Cryptographic architectures can basically convey the journalistic five Ws and H questions: **who** uses the keys, **what** are the key types, **why** keys are used, **where** keys are stored, **when** keys are used, and **how** keys are used.

- Who uses the keys: identifies the entity, whether it be an individual, mobile device, laptop, server, network appliance, or an application.
- What are the key types: defines the symmetric or asymmetric algorithm and key sizes.
- Why keys are used: conveys the security purpose such as encryption, authentication, integrity, non-repudiation, or tokenization.
- Where keys are stored: captures location information, such as on the Internet, within a DMZ or on an internal network.
- When keys are used: provides cryptographic protocol information, such as authentication, encryption, or key establishment.
- How keys are used: gives further detail regarding key usage within a cryptographic protocol such as TLS cipher suites.

Cryptography information might be documented using diagrams or other formats such as lists, tables, or other spreadsheets. While lists are valuable they do not provide a visual perspective; literally a picture is worth a thousand words. An existing application or network diagram might be reused, or a specialized illustration can be developed. For example, Figure 6.8 shows an application architecture with cryptography information.

The Web servers have TLS keys, a private asymmetric key and a public key certificate, for the external HTTPS connection to web browsers. Since browsers do not offer client certificates, the Web servers send their server certificates to the browser as part of the TLS handshake to establish the symmetric session keys. The browser needs to validate the Web App certificate, including the certificate chain to the trust anchor, as indicated by the certificate loops.

The Web servers also store salted and hashed passwords for individual authentication and authorization. However, no keys are used. The passwords entered by the individuals using their browsers are transmitted over the HTTPS connection, salted and hashed by the Web servers, and then matched to the stored versions for password verification.

The BP servers have TLS keys, another private asymmetric key and a public key certificate, for the external TLS connection to the BA servers. Likewise, the BA servers likewise have TLS keys, a private asymmetric key and a public key certificate, for mutual authentication. Both servers exchange TLS certificates to establish the symmetric session keys. Further, both servers need to validate each other's TLS certificates, including the certificate chains to a trust anchor. Note that the two certificate chains might very well validate to different trust anchors.

The App servers have TLS keys, a private asymmetric key and a public key certificate, for the internal TLS connections to the Web servers and the BP servers. The Web servers and the BP servers reuse their same certificates for both their external and internal TLS connections. Thus, the TLS connections between the App-to-Web servers and App-to-BP servers have mutual authentication. Further, all of the servers need to validate the exchanged certificates including the certificate chain to a trust anchor. Because the Web and BP certificates are also used for external connections, whereas the App certificates are only used for internal connections, the App certificates might validate to different trust anchors.

The DB servers do not have any TLS keys, as the internal connections to the App servers are not over a secure channel. However, a security professional should be able to argue that while the connections are over a private network, the sensitivity of the data transmitted between the App and DB servers and the relative risks of an unauthenticated connections warrant a TLS connection. Regardless, the DB server has a symmetric key for database encryption (DBE).

Adding cryptography information to the application architecture in Figure 6.8 is meaningful and helpful to understand the cryptographic architecture. The entities (who) are identified, the key types (what) and purposes (why) are implied by the protocols (HTTP, TLS), the locations (where) are indicated, and the protocols (when) are provided. But not all of the connections are included, and the cryptographic details (how) are not captured in the improved application architecture diagram. However, the application team might not necessarily know the network or cryptographic details, so further review by the security professional is needed. Additional examples for network architecture are shown in Figures 6.9 and 6.10.

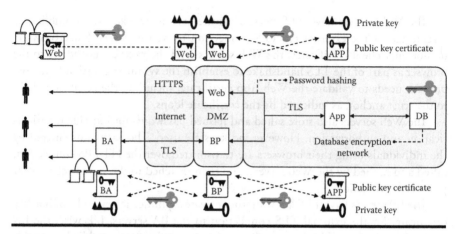

Figure 6.9   Application architecture with crypto.

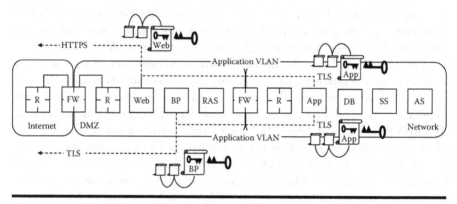

Figure 6.10   Network architecture for application VLAN.

Figure 6.9 shows a network architecture for the application VLAN with cryptography information. The application VLAN in the DMZ restricts access to the Web and BP servers, and another application VLAN in the network limits access to the App and DB servers. As discussed for the DMZ application VLAN:

- The Web servers have TLS keys, a private asymmetric key and a public key certificate, for the external HTTPS connection to web browsers.
- The App servers have TLS keys, a private asymmetric key and a public key certificate, for the internal TLS connections to the Web servers and the BP servers.

As observed for the network application VLAN:

- The App servers have TLS keys, a private asymmetric key and a public key certificate, for the internal TLS connections to the Web servers and the BP servers.

- The Web servers and the BP servers reuse their same certificates for both their external and internal TLS connections.

Modifying network diagrams with cryptography information likewise is helpful to understand the cryptographic architecture. The network devices (who) are identified, the key types (what) and purposes (why) are implied by the protocols (HTTP, TLS), the locations (where) are indicated, and the protocols (when) are provided. However, Figure 6.9 does not document all of the connections; for a more complete viewpoint, Figure 6.10 needs to be considered.

Figure 6.10 shows a network architecture for the administrative VLAN with cryptography information. The admin VLAN in the DMZ limits access to the RAS and a separate VLAN in the network restricts access to the SS and AS. From a network perspective,

- Outside the DMZ the Internet routers have IPsec keys, a private asymmetric key and a public key certificate, for cross-connecting the East and West datacenters.
- Inside the DMZ the RAS has TLS keys, a private asymmetric key and a public key certificate, for VPN access.
- Inside the network the routers have IPsec keys, a private asymmetric key and a public key certificate, for synchronizing the DB servers.
- Inside the network the AS has TLS keys, a private asymmetric key and a public key certificate, for connecting to the RAS inside the DMZ.
- Inside the network the AS has SSH keys, a private asymmetric key and a public key certificate, for administrating other servers and network devices.

As mentioned, updating network diagrams with cryptography information is helpful to understand the cryptographic architecture. The network devices (who) are identified, the key types (what) and purposes (why) are implied by the protocols (HTTP, TLS), the locations (where) are indicated, and the protocols (when) are provided. However, Figures 6.10 and 6.11 together still do not address all of the cryptography information. Another viewpoint is adding cryptography information to the data diagram as shown in Figure 6.12.

- The web servers have a TLS certificate chain and its TLS private key for external connections, along with an SSH public key for internal administration.
- The BP servers have a TLS certificate chain and its TLS private key for external connections, along with an SSH public key for internal administration.
- The RASs have a TLS certificate chain and its TLS private key for internal connections, along with an SSH public key for internal administration.
- The App servers have a TLS certificate chain and its TLS private key for external connections, along with an SSH public key for internal administration.

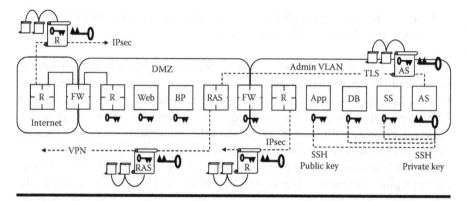

Figure 6.11   Network architecture for admin VLAN.

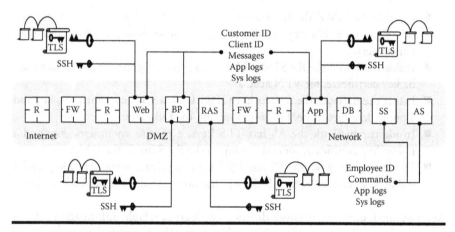

Figure 6.12   Data diagram with crypto information.

However, even this perspective only provides partial crypto info. The protocols (e.g., HTTPS, VPN, IPsec) are not documented, and the datacenter connections are not included. Hence, a specialized diagram should be considered for documenting a cryptographic architecture such as the example provided in Figure 6.13. The locations and connections shown are based on the application and network diagrams but consolidated to reflect cryptography information.

For Figure 6.13, each of the cryptography instances are numbered for cross-referencing. Asymmetric key pairs for HTTPS, TLS, and IPsec are reflected by a private key and either a public key or a public key certificate. Asymmetric SSH public keys are shown for most servers and routers, where the SSH private keys reside on the AS. Asymmetric ephemeral key pairs and symmetric session keys are not shown as they are temporary; however, the symmetric DBE is included.

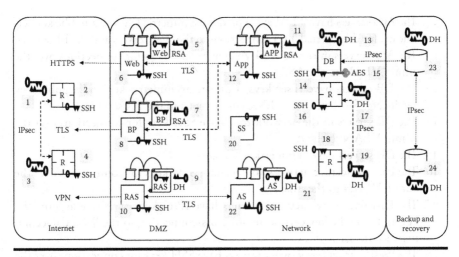

Figure 6.13 Cryptographic architecture.

1. The East datacenter Internet routers have IPsec keys, a private asymmetric key and a public key certificate, for cross-connecting to the West datacenter Internet routers.
2. The East datacenter Internet routers have SSH keys for connections over the admin VLAN to the ASs.
3. The West datacenter Internet routers have IPsec keys, a private asymmetric key and a public key certificate, for cross-connecting to the East datacenter Internet routers.
4. The West datacenter Internet routers have SSH keys for connections over the admin VLAN to the ASs.
5. The Web servers in the DMZ have TLS keys, a private asymmetric key and a public key certificate, for external HTTPS connections to web browsers, and for internal TLS connections to the App servers.
6. The Web servers in the DMZ have SSH keys for connections over the admin VLAN to the ASs.
7. The BP servers in the DMZ have TLS keys, a private asymmetric key and a public key certificate, for external TLS connections (e.g., BA servers) and for internal TLS connections to the App servers.
8. The BP servers in the DMZ have SSH keys for connections over the admin VLAN to the ASs.
9. The RASs in the DMZ have TLS keys, a private asymmetric key and a public key certificate, for external VPN connections and for internal TLS connections to the ASs.
10. The RASs in the DMZ have SSH keys for connections over the admin VLAN to the ASs.

11. The App servers have TLS keys, a private asymmetric key and a public key certificate, for the internal TLS connections to the Web servers and the BP servers.
12. The App servers in the network zone have SSH keys for connections over the admin VLAN to the ASs.
13. The DB servers have IPsec keys, a private asymmetric key and a public key certificate, for the external IPsec connections to the BR servers.
14. The DB servers in the network zone have SSH keys for connections over the admin VLAN to the ASs.
15. The DB servers have symmetric DBE keys.
16. The East datacenter network routers have SSH keys for connections over the admin VLAN to the ASs.
17. The East datacenter network routers have IPsec keys, a private asymmetric key and a public key certificate, for cross-connecting to the West datacenter network routers.
18. The West datacenter network routers have SSH keys for connections over the admin VLAN to the ASs.
19. The West datacenter network routers have IPsec keys, a private asymmetric key and a public key certificate, for cross-connecting to the East datacenter network routers.
20. The SSs in the network zone have SSH keys for connections over the admin VLAN to the ASs.
21. The ASs in the network zone have TLS keys, a private asymmetric key and a public key certificate, for internal TLS connections to the RASs.
22. The ASs in the network zone have SSH keys for connections over the admin VLAN to the other servers in the DMZ, network zone, and routers.
23. The West BR servers have IPsec keys, a private asymmetric key and a public key certificate, for synchronizing to the East BR servers.
24. The East BR servers have IPsec keys, a private asymmetric key and a public key certificate, for synchronizing to the West BR servers.

There are almost four dozen keys shown in Figure 6.13, counting symmetric keys, asymmetric public keys and digital certificates, and asymmetric private keys. The graphical depiction gives an overview and the relative relations between the keys. However, it cannot provide all of the associated information, as there is simply insufficient room to include everything. Another option might be cross-referencing the graphical depiction with an inventory. But, an inventory without the graphic is less meaningful; having both are optimal.

6.5 Cryptographic Inventory

In addition to the cryptographic architecture diagram provided in Figure 6.13, more information can be proved such as an inventory shown in Table 6.2. The basic

Table 6.2 Cryptographic Architecture Inventory

#	Who Entity	What Algorithm	Why Purpose	Where Location	When Protocol	How Details
1	Router	DHE	Encryption	Internet	IPsec	ESP
2	Router	RSA	Authentication	Internet	SSH	Digital signature
3	Router	DH	Encryption	Internet	IPsec	ESP
4	Router	RSA	Authentication	Internet	SSH	Digital signature
5	Web	RSA	Encryption	DMZ	HTTPS	Key transport
6	Web	RSA	Authentication	DMZ	SSH	Digital signature
7	BP	RSA	Encryption	DMZ	TLS	Key transport
8	BP	RSA	Authentication	DMZ	SSH	Digital signature
9	RAS	DHE	Encryption	DMZ	TLS	Key agreement
10	RAS	RSA	Authentication	DMZ	SSH	Digital signature
11	App	RSA	Encryption	Network	TLS	Key transport
12	App	RSA	Authentication	Network	SSH	Digital signature
13	DB	DHE	Encryption	Network	IPsec	Key agreement
14	DB	RSA	Authentication	Network	SSH	Digital signature

(Continued)

Table 6.2 (Continued) Cryptographic Architecture Inventory

#	Who Entity	What Algorithm	Why Purpose	Where Location	When Protocol	How Details
15	DB	AES	Encryption	Network	DBE	Encryption
16	Router	RSA	Authentication	Network	SSH	Digital signature
17	Router	DH	Encryption	Network	IPsec	Key agreement
18	Router	RSA	Authentication	Network	SSH	Digital signature
19	Router	DH	Encryption	Network	IPsec	Key agreement
20	SS	RSA	Authentication	Network	SSH	Digital signature
21	AS	RSA	Encryption	Network	TLS	Key transport
22	AS	RSA	Authentication	Network	SSH	Digital signature
23	BUR	DH	Encryption	BUR	IPsec	Key agreement
24	BUR	DH	Encryption	BUR	IPsec	Key agreement

EPS, encapsulating security payload; DH, Diffie–Hellman; DHE, Diffie–Hellman ephemeral; BUR, backup & recovery.

five Ws and H questions can be summarized using a simple table. There is a practical limit as to how much information can be provided in a diagram. Too much information clutters the diagram and makes it unreadable, whereas too little information reduces its usefulness. Some graphical tools allow embedded comments or attachments, but this only allows a reader to see one instance at a time. A table allows a reader to see common data points or data patterns.

Table 6.2 is numbered per the cryptographic architecture diagram in Figure 6.13. The basic five Ws and H questions are provided in each row. The entity (who) information can be as detailed as needed; it might be host name specific. The algorithm (what) information can be extended to include the key size (e.g., Rivest–Shamir–Adleman (RSA) 2048-bit, Advanced Encryption Standard (AES) 256-bit). The purpose (why) can be enhanced to reflect application or network specific uses. The location (where) might be expanded to include physical address (e.g., 123 Main Street) or an IP address. The protocol (when) might include protocol options or specific configurations. Further details (how) might include processing restrictions, error handling, legal warranties or liabilities, or other business-related manners.

Alternatively, a metadata structure defined using Abstract Syntax Notation One (ASN.1) can be used to encode the associated information for each cryptographic module. Refer to Annex: ASN.1 Module for a complete section suitable for input to programming language code generation tools. The abstract schema might be used to populate a database or create a graphic interpretation of the cryptographic module information.

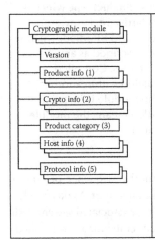

Each cryptographic module can be defined using six data elements. Simple elements are denoted as single boxes, whereas complex elements are shown as three boxes. The complex elements indicate one or more occurrences of the data element. Thus, the primary element **Cryptographic Module** is itself a complex structure that can occur more than once. The primary elements can be stored in a database or list of all cryptographic modules which can define the cryptographic architecture. The ASN.1 module in this book might be parsed and a graphics engine might be used to create a diagram as shown in Figure 6.13 discussed earlier.

Version identifies the ASN.1 module release number. For the purposes of this book, the version number is zero "0" for the structure provided in Annex: ASN.1 Module. Any modifications or updates should increment the version number.

This allows the syntax to be programmatically parsed and interpreted for displaying information or analyzing architectures.

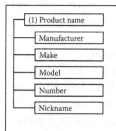

Product Info (1) is defined as **Product Data** which is a sequence of one or more **Product Name** consisting of five data elements: Manufacturer, Make, Model, Number, and Nickname. The manufacturer name, along with the equipment make and model, might be sufficient to uniquely identify the cryptographic module. The manufacturer number provides further details. Nickname allows for quick reference.

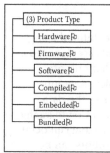

Crypto Info (2) is defined as **Crypto Data** which a sequence of one or more **Crypto Name** consisting of five other data elements: Algorithm ID, Key Size Bits, Hash Size Bits, Key Use, and Key Lifecycle. The ID defines the cryptographic algorithm, sizes are expressed as the number of bits, and key use is a sequence of object identifiers (OIDs). The key lifecycle (6) is a sequence of dates.

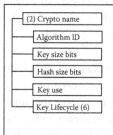

Product Category (3) is defined as **Product Type** which is a sequence of Boolean flags: Hardware, Firmware, Software, Complied, Embedded, and Bundled. Thus, a cryptographic module can be described as any combination of these characteristics. Compiled means the module is encapsulated within another product. Embedded means the module is installed within another product. Bundled means the module is available with another product.

Host Info (4) is defined as **Host Data** which is another sequence of one or more **Product Name** consisting of five data elements: Manufacturer, Make, Model, Number, and Nickname. The host information identifies the associated system with which the cryptographic module is connected, complied, embedded, or bundled. For example, a HSM might have a network connection or physically cabled to a server. As another example, a cryptographic module might be embedded within a network appliance. Alternatively, a cryptographic library might be complied into an application or bundled with an operating system.

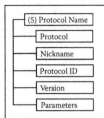

Protocol Info (5) is defined as **Protocol Data** which is a sequence of one or more **Protocol Name** consisting of five data elements: Protocol, Nickname, ID, Version, and Parameters. Protocols have names (e.g., TLS) and nicknames (e.g., TLS), identifiers (e.g., OID), versions (e.g., v1.2), and sometimes parameters that provide further information.

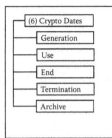

Key Lifecycle (6) is defined as **Crypto Data** consisting of five date and time stages: Generation, Use, End, Terminate, and Archive. Generation is when the key was created. Use is when the key is valid. End is when the key is no longer valid. Termination is when the key must be destroyed. Archive is when the key is no longer kept for verification past its end or termination dates.

In conclusion, any development project produces artifacts such as an application or network architectures, but all too often the cryptographic architecture is overlooked. Modern-day networks, systems, and products have evolved with cryptography almost everywhere, but details are often overlooked, undocumented, or simply ignored. All too often, application developers, technical managers, and business analysts simply hope for the best. When vulnerabilities affect cryptographic algorithms or protocols, the architectural impacts are unknown. Consequently, the critical nature of the cryptographic architecture needs to be included by security professionals.

Chapter 7

Risk Management

Risk management is based on the presumption that data risks can be reduced by implementing security controls. While this is generally true, there are limits and trade-offs as to what can be achieved with regard to cryptographic architectures. Figure 7.1 shows a risk model with a descending risk reduction curve. The x-axis represents security controls increasing from left to right, and the y-axis represents data risks decreasing from top to bottom. The curve does not actually touch the y-axis (near the x–y origin) because every system and network has some minimal security controls (e.g., access controls, event logging) that help reduce risk. As increasing security controls (moving left to right along the x-axis) reduce risk, the distance between the curve and the x-axis represents the residual risk. However, the curve never reaches the x-axis as there are always some residual risks.

The goal, of course, is to achieve the lowest reasonable risk with the fewest security controls that cost the least amount of resources to save money. This is sometimes called the Magic Box that represents sufficiently low risk with acceptable security controls. For example, if the probability of a successful attack is considered too remote, or the impact to business is viewed minimal, the security controls are less likely to be implemented, especially of the security control is costly and disproportional to the value of the application and its data. Conversely, if the benefit of the security control such as reduced risk or regulatory compliance is sufficiently high and the overall cost is acceptable and proportional to the application (and its data), the security control is more likely to be implemented. The ISO/IEC Code of Practice for Information Security Management standard [74] recommends that information security policy document approved by management incorporates a framework for setting control objectives and controls, including the structure of risk assessment and risk management. An example framework is the Risk Management Framework for the Federal Information Security Management Act provides a six-step process [75].

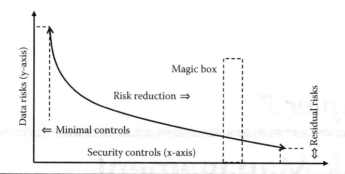

Figure 7.1 Risk reduction curve.

1. **Categorize** the information system and the information processed, stored, and transmitted by that system based on an impact analysis. This step, including consideration of legislation, policies, directives, regulations, standards, and organizational mission/business/operational requirements, facilitates the identification of security requirements.
2. **Select** an initial set of baseline security controls for the information system based on the security categorization; tailoring and supplementing the security control baseline as needed based on an organizational assessment of risk and local conditions.
3. **Implement** the security controls and describe how the controls are employed within the information system and its environment of operation.
4. **Assess** the security controls using appropriate assessment procedures to determine the extent to which the controls are implemented correctly, operating as intended, and producing the desired outcome with respect to meeting the security requirements for the system.
5. **Authorize** information system operation based on a determination of the risk to organizational operations and assets, individuals, other organizations, and the nation resulting from the operation of the information system and the decision that this risk is acceptable.
6. **Monitor** the security controls in the information system on an ongoing basis including assessing control effectiveness, documenting changes to the system or its environment of operation, conducting security impact analyses of the associated changes, and reporting the security state of the system to designated organizational officials.

However, it is often difficult to implement or measure one security control that does not affect or rely on other controls. For example, imposing a password construction rule (e.g., eight characters consisting of both uppercase and lowercase letters with at least one number and one special character) actually reduces the set of possible passwords. At the same time, no password construction rules allow users to choose poor and easily guessable passwords. Thus, adding a password construction control affects the password authentication control. But rarely does any security control operate in a vacuum, see Figure 7.2 for a security model. The aggregate security needs to be understood to determine the overall risks versus controls.

Figure 7.2 shows a layered "onion" approach to evaluate risk and controls. Cryptographic keys are used to protect data. Cryptographic modules are used to protect cryptographic keys. But a cryptographic module might be a software library bundled with a computer system, embedded within application software, or enclosed within a cryptographic hardware security module (HSM). Regardless, systems protect cryptographic modules. And ultimately, facilities with physical and logical security controls protect systems. However, with respect to cryptographic architectures, there is an intrinsic standards gap, shown in Figure 7.3.

When a standard for a cryptographic algorithm, key management scheme, or security protocol is published, it will contain requirements (e.g., shall) and recommendations (e.g., should) that the reader is expected to understand. Unfortunately, when such a security standard is productized there is often a gap between what the standard says versus what the product does. This is due to a variety of factors including lack of understanding, lack of knowledge, lack of expertise, design flaws, coding errors, cost limitations, and time to market. Today's information

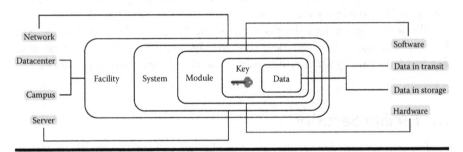

Figure 7.2   Security model.

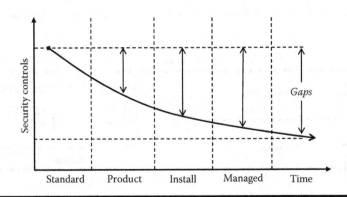

Figure 7.3   Standards gaps.

technology industry tends to push products to market faster with less testing such that bug fixes, patches, and frequent modifications are now a common theme. Unfortunately, this is often true for cryptographic products whose updates can sometimes adversely affect security controls.

Another gap source is the installation of cryptographic products. When a cryptographic product is misconfigured, its security can be compromised. Some products support older algorithms, weaker keys, or aging protocols, for backwards compatibility. If the unwanted offerings cannot be disabled but just not used, the vulnerable methods might be inadvertently or intentionally be used, increasing risk to the application environment. Further, if the product is used in a manner inconsistent with the corresponding standard or the manufacturer's recommendation, it can increase risk. For example, a cryptographic product intended to encrypt data but instead is used to encrypt keys increases the risk of a key compromise.

Once a product is installed, it needs to be properly managed. Access controls need to be in place to avoid unauthorized re-configurations. Bug fixes, patches, and modification need to be applied but only after the updates have fully tested in a nonproduction environment. Processing needs to be monitored to ensure no attacks are active. Configuration changes, software changes, and processing all need to be logged, and the logs need to be analyzed. However, if the product is improperly managed the gap might increase risk, and over time the gap might increase.

The following sections discuss each of the layers: Facility Security, System Security Cryptographic Modules, Key Management, and Data Management. The first layer Facility Security discusses physical and logical security controls.

7.1 Facility Security

Facility security includes a wide variety of physical and logical controls to protect systems, which in turn protect cryptographic modules, which protect cryptographic keys, which are used to protect data. Figure 7.4 illustrates an example datacenter surrounded by a security fence and encircled by a drainage ditch. A single entrance

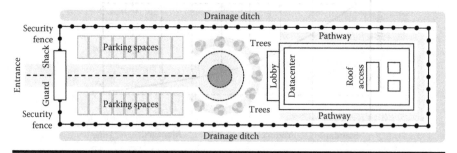

Figure 7.4   Physical security.

with a guard shack provides ingress and egress to the campus. Between the parking spaces and the lobby entrance is a circular drive enclosed by trees planted on a berm. The building has roof access and is surrounded by a pathway.

The physical security controls afforded by the numerous campus elements represent a layered security approach. The various controls provided by each element are presented from the campus exterior toward the interior into the actual datacenter.

- The drainage ditch around the facility not only prevents flooding during heavy rains, it also acts as an "invisible" barrier obstructing vehicles from crashing the security fence.
- The security fence surrounding the facility hinders unauthorized individuals from entering the facility by directing traffic to the single entrance.
- The guard shack at the entrance controls inbound and outbound vehicle traffic and the guards authenticate and authorize employees and visitors.
- The landscaped trees and the raised berm is another "invisible" barrier blocking vehicle access to the building lobby.
- The pathway around the building allows guards to patrol the grounds.
- The lobby at the building entrance controls entering and departing human traffic and the guards authenticate and authorize visitors.

Cameras monitor traffic at the guard shack, the parking lot area, the lobby, the pathway, the foot traffic in the lobby, and the rooftop access. In addition to the physical security controls, there are logical security controls such as automated processes and manual procedures that supplement the overall security posture.

- At the entrance, the guards must recognize employees but check identification of any unfamiliar faces including all visitors. Visitors must be invited by an employee.
- In the lobby, guards issue visitor badges and manage employee escorts. Employees' badges are scanned by readers for access through mantraps into the main building.
- Within the main building, employees regularly display badges and escort visitors at all times. Some areas require badge access and visitor sign in.

Camera video and badge access logs are retained in case of a security incident. Some videos are kept online for quick reference, while others are preserved offline for longer periods. Guards patrol the pathway and the rooftop to inspect the building. Problems are reported and repairs are effected straightaway. Videos and logs are reviewed regularly for continuity. Any abnormality or suspicious activity is immediately reported. From a cryptographic architecture perspective, the physical and logical controls to restrict access to cryptographic equipment, systems that employ cryptography, and the storage of cryptographic material is an important group of compensating controls. The next layer System Security discusses business continuity and disaster recovery (BCDR), vulnerability lifecycle management systems (VLMSs), and penetration (pen) testing.

7.2 System Security

BCDR was introduced in Chapter 6 when discussing the datacenter diagram and the cryptographic architecture. The datacenter diagram recognized that Internet connections were redundant between the regional west and east datacenters, data was backed up for recovery, and data was synchronized between the two datacenters and the two backup and recovery sites. The cryptographic architecture identified the Internet cross-connection, the datacenter cross-connections, the backup connection, and the backup and recovery cross-connection. BCDR includes processes, procedures, and people to maintain business availability and recover information in the event of a disaster.

VLMS maintain software for applications, servers, and other network devices. When a bug fix, patch, or modification is provided by the product manufacturer, the changes need to be applied. National Institute of Standards and Technology (NIST) provides a guide to enterprise patch management technologies [76] for identifying, acquiring, installing, and verifying patches. The guideline discusses challenges inherent in performing patch management and provides an overview of technologies. There are various VLMS models. For example, the Qualys paper, a Guide to Effective Remediation of Network Vulnerabilities, provides an eight-step process [77].

1. Create security policies and controls
2. Track inventory/categorize assets
3. Scan systems for vulnerabilities
4. Compare vulnerabilities against inventory
5. Classify risks
6. Pretest patches
7. Apply patches
8. Re-scan and confirm fixes

As another example, the System Admin, Audit, Network, Security (SANS) paper Implementing a Vulnerability Management Process describes a simpler five-phase program [78]. The SANS first preparation phase basically combines the first two Qualys steps. Both models recognize vulnerability scanning; Qualys step three and SANS phase three. The Qualys steps five, six, and seven are essentially merged into the SANS fourth phase. Both models recommend re-scans to confirm the fixes.

1. Preparation
2. Vulnerability scan

3. Define remediating actions
4. Implement remediating actions
5. Re-scan

Similarly, the X9.111 standard [79] identifies five stages for penetration testing. Whereas a vulnerability scan is a test process that attempts to identify the presence of potential vulnerabilities to known network-based attacks; a penetration test attempts to exploit vulnerabilities to determine whether unauthorized access or other malicious activity is possible. Penetration testing includes network and application testing as well as controls and processes around the networks and applications, and occurs from both outside the network trying to come in (external testing) and from inside the network.

1. Specification of penetration test
2. Engagement guidelines
3. Penetration test activity
4. Engagement reporting
5. Remediation

The first stage is to identify and evaluate the set of information security objectives agreed to in the statement of work. The second stage is to arrive at an agreement on the test parameters and scope. The third stage is when the actual penetration test activity occurs. The fourth stage is for the tester reports findings to the organization. The fifth stage is remediation either independent of the tester or if the tester is involved, the same tester cannot conduct follow-up tests. From a cryptographic architecture perspective, BCDR and VLMS along with pen testing are important aspects to ensure reliability of cryptographic equipment, systems that employ cryptography, and the storage of cryptographic material. The next layer Cryptographic Modules addresses hardware versus software cryptography and network security for using and managing cryptographic modules.

7.3 Cryptographic Modules

A cryptographic module provides cryptographic services by executing cryptographic algorithms (e.g., encryption, Message Authentication Code (MAC), keyed Hash Message Authentication Code [HMAC], digital signatures) and protecting cryptographic keys during the algorithm execution. Cryptographic modules also perform related functions (e.g., hash, number generations) that do not use keys. In order for a cryptographic algorithm to use a key, the key must be cleartext. The key might be encrypted using another key, called a key encryption key (KEK), to protect it during storage or transmission, but it must be decrypted for the algorithm execution in memory. See Figure 7.5 for an example of cryptographic module.

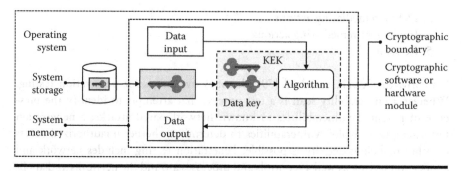

Figure 7.5   Internal cryptographic module.

Figure 7.5 shows an internal cryptographic module residing within the system memory of a computer that is controlled by an operating system. The algorithm executes within the memory of the cryptographic module. The data key is stored encrypted in system storage. The encrypted data key is fetched from storage and transmitted to the cryptographic module where it is decrypted using the KEK. The cleartext KEK and cleartext data key never leave the memory of the module. The cleartext data key can now be used with the algorithm.

Figure 7.5 also shows the data input and data output into and out of the algorithm. The input data is moved from system memory to the module memory so it can be operated on by the algorithm and data key, and the output data is moved from the module memory to the system memory. For example, the input data might be cleartext that gets encrypted by the algorithm and key such that the output data is ciphertext. Conversely, the input data might be ciphertext that gets decrypted by the algorithm and key such that the output data is cleartext.

If the cryptographic module is software based then the module memory is the same as the system member which means the cleartext KEK and cleartext data key are vulnerable. However, if the cryptographic module is hardware based then the module memory is separate from the system member which means the KEK and data key are never exposed outside the cryptographic module. In general, cryptographic hardware modules are designed to protect keys and only allow cleartext data to be inputted and outputted.

Figure 7.6 shows an external cryptographic hardware module connected to a network, often called a HSM or a secure cryptographic device (SCD). Similar to the internal module, the algorithm executes within the cryptographic boundary. The encrypted data key is transmitted to the module where it is decrypted using the cleartext KEK. The cleartext KEK and cleartext data key never leave the cryptographic boundary. Also shown are the data input and data output which are likewise transmitted, typically over a secure network connection between the application system and the cryptographic module. The secure network connections typically use transport layer security (TLS) or equivalent cryptographic protocol. The HSM is often its own public key infrastructure such that the cryptographic module

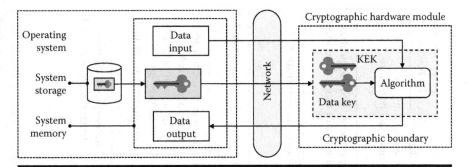

Figure 7.6 External cryptographic module.

is the root certification authority (CA) issuing TLS server certificates to itself and TLS client certificates to application systems.

NIST [80] defines a cryptographic module as the set of hardware, software, and/or firmware that implements approved security functions (including cryptographic algorithms and key generation) and is contained within the cryptographic boundary. NIST further defines a cryptographic boundary as an explicitly defined continuous perimeter that establishes the physical bounds of a cryptographic module and contains all the hardware, software, and/or firmware components of a cryptographic module. The NIST standard defines requirements for 11 security areas with four different security levels summarized in Table 7.1.

Security Level 1 is the lowest level of security, allowing software (or firmware) components of a cryptographic module executed on a general purpose computing system using an unevaluated operating system. However, one benefit is that approved algorithms (or security functions) are included. Approval means that algorithms have been evaluated to be correctly implemented per the corresponding standards, such as the symmetric algorithm advanced encryption standard (AES) [81]. Thus, vulnerabilities due to weak algorithms or buggy software are avoided.

Security Level 2 enhances level 1 with tamper-evident mechanisms, role-based authentication (RBA), and an evaluated operating system. Tamper-evident mechanisms for hardware include visible coatings, observable seals, pick-resistant locks, and removable covers. Software integrity mechanisms might include MAC, HMAC, or digital signatures for code signing. RBA means the cryptographic module authenticates the authorization of an operator to assume a specific role (e.g., end user, key manager, administrator) and perform a corresponding set of services. An evaluated operating system means it has been assessed using a Common Criteria [82] Protection Profile (PP) at evaluation assurance level two (EAL2).

Security Level 3 increases level 2 by adding tamper detect and tamper response mechanisms, identity-based authentication, dedicated input/output ports, and evaluated EAL3 (or higher) operating system. Recognition of unauthorized physical access triggers key zeroization; on detection, the module erases the cryptographic keys. Authentication verifies that the identified operator is authorized to access a

Table 7.1 NIST Summary of Security Requirements

	Security Area	Security Level 1	Security Level 2	Security Level 3	Security Level 4
1	Cryptographic module specification	Specification of cryptographic module, cryptographic boundary, approved algorithms, and approved modes of operation. Description of cryptographic module, including all hardware, software, and firmware components. Statement of module security policy.			
2	Cryptographic module ports and interfaces	Required and optional interfaces. Specification of all interfaces and of all input and output data paths.		Data ports for unprotected CSPs logically or physically separated from other data ports.	
3	Roles, services, and authentication	Logical separation of required and optional roles and services.	Role-based or identity-based operator authentication.	Identity-based operator authentication.	
4	Finite state model	Specification of finite state model. Required states and optional states. State transition diagram and specification of state transitions.			
5	Physical security	Production grade equipment.	Locks or tamper evidence.	Tamper detection and response for covers and doors.	Tamper detection and response envelope. Environmental failure protection or environmental failure testing.
6	Operational environment	Single operator. Executable code. Approved integrity technique.	Referenced PPs evaluated at EAL2 with specified discretionary access control mechanisms and auditing.	Referenced PPs plus trusted path evaluated at EAL3 plus security policy modeling.	Referenced PPs plus trusted path evaluated at AL4.

(Continued)

Table 7.1 (Continued)   NIST Summary of Security Requirements

	Security Area	Security Level 1	Security Level 2	Security Level 3	Security Level 4
7	Cryptographic key management	Key management mechanisms: random number and key generation, key establishment, key distribution, key entry/output, key storage, and key zeroization.			
8	EMI/EMC	47 CFR FCC Part 15. Subpart B, Class A (Business use). Applicable FCC requirements (for radio).		47 CFR FCC Part 15. Subpart B, Class B (Home use).	
9	Self-tests	Power-up tests: cryptographic algorithm tests, software/firmware integrity tests, critical functions tests. Conditional tests.			
10	Design assurance	Configuration management (CM). Secure installation and generation. Design and policy correspondence. Guidance documents.	CM system. Secure distribution. Functional specification.	High-level language implementation.	Formal model. Detailed explanations (informal proofs). Preconditions and postconditions.
11	Mitigation of other attacks	Specification of mitigation of attacks for which no testable requirements are currently available.			

specific role and perform a corresponding set of services. Dedicated ports require that the import or export of cleartext critical security parameters (CSPs) such as key components be physically or logically separated from other ports. The operating system needs to be assessed against a Common Criteria [82] PP at EAL3.

Security Level 4 is the highest level of security improving level 3 by requiring stronger anti-tamper mechanisms, environmental sensors, and evaluated EAL4 (or higher). Detection of any physical penetration triggers key zeroization. Environmental sensors verify that the module is used within its normal operating ranges (e.g., voltage, temperature, vibration) to thwart attacks. The operating system needs to be assessed using a Common Criteria [82] PP at EAL4.

Table 7.1 shows the increasing Security Area requirements for each Security Level, but some of the areas are the same for more than one level. For example, Security Area (1) Cryptographic Module Specification has the same documentation requirement for all four levels. Conversely, Security Area (2) Cryptography Module Ports and Interfaces has the same requirements for levels 1 and 2 but separates data ports for CSPs for levels 3 and 4. As another example, Security Area (5) Physical Security increases requirements for each Security Level. Figure 7.7 provides a graphical summary of the Table 7.1 requirements.

The NIST standard has also been translated into an international standard [83], and the American National Standards Institute (ANSI) [84] standard defines an SCD as a device that provides physically and logically protected cryptographic services and storage, for example, personal identification number (PIN) entry device or HSM. However, only NIST provides a cryptographic module validation program[*]

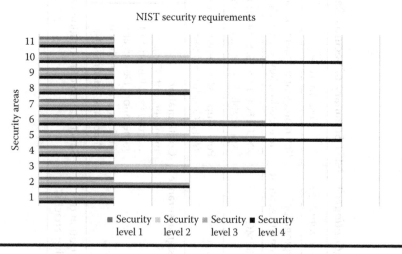

Figure 7.7 NIST security requirements.

---

and a cryptographic algorithm validation program* for the algorithms it recognizes. The National Information Assurance Partnership[†] (NIAP) is a partnership between the NIST and the National Security Agency to support the Common Criteria Evaluation and Validation Scheme. The Common Criteria [82] provides a method to define security requirements for the evaluation of products. Requirements are published as either a PP by an independent standards organization or a Security Target typically provided by the product manufacturer. NIAP maintains a list[‡] of approved PPs; however, notably there are no PPs for cryptographic modules.

From a cryptographic architecture viewpoint, standards-based cryptography is preferred over proprietary solutions. However, different algorithms and other cryptography requirements will vary worldwide, and some countries will mandate algorithms. Further, cryptographic modules evaluated by an independent authoritative organization (e.g., NIST) are preferred. Modules with NIST certification have evaluated cryptographic algorithms (at least those approved by NIST) and provide a security profile. Security profiles identify all cryptographic algorithms, key lengths, hash lengths, and security protocols; a valuable source of accurate and reliable cryptographic information. The next layer Key Management discusses key lifecycle.

7.4 Key Management

Cryptographic keys, including symmetric keys, asymmetric key pairs, and related cryptographic material all need to be managed safely and securely over their lifecycle. The key lifecycle stages differ between standards and among organizations, but for this book, the ANSI X9.79 [85] key lifecycle is provided in Figure 7.8. Six stages are recognized: (1) key generation, (2) key distribution, (3) key usage, (4) key

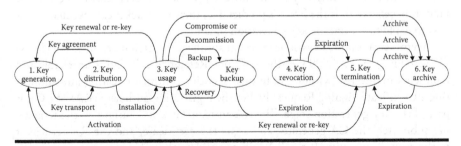

Figure 7.8   Key management lifecycle.

---

* https://csrc.nist.gov/projects/cryptographic-algorithm-validation-program

† www.niap-ccevs.org/

‡ www.niap-ccevs.org/Profile/PP.cfm

revocation, (5) key termination, and (6) key archive. Without proper controls, keys are at risk of compromise at any lifecycle stage.

- Symmetric keys might be disclosed allowing encrypted data to be revealed or data to be modified or substituted.
- Asymmetric private keys might be disclosed allowing encrypted cryptographic material to be revealed or creating fraudulent digital signatures.
- Asymmetric public keys might be substituted allowing various man-in-the-middle (MITM) attacks. Digital signatures might be similarly substituted or encrypted keying material can be revealed.

Relative risks are discussed for each key management lifecycle stage. While some risks are more theoretical than others, actual real-world attacks are also reviewed. For some case studies, the risk scenario is provided but the names are kept anonymous.

Key generation occurs when the keys are created. Symmetric keys are generated using random number generators (RNGs) [86] and [89] or pseudo-random number generators (PRNGs) [88]. An RNG needs a good source of entropy [87], so the randomness is truly random. Otherwise, if the entropy source is vulnerable to outside influence, the symmetric key or at least some of its bits might be predictable. An attacker can use such predictability to reduce the possible key space for an exhaustive attack, such as the Return of the Coppersmith Attack identified in the Common Vulnerabilities and Exposure (CVE-2017-15361*) notice. Similarly, a PRNG relies on an RNG for a random input. Alternatively, the PRNG might be used with the same keying material to establish the same symmetric key more than once or at different locations.

Asymmetric keys are generated in pairs, the private key and the public key, and rely not only on random numbers but also prime number generators (PNGs) [90]. Random numbers can be tested for primality using probabilistic testing, or prime number can be constructively built. However, prime numbers likewise need to be randomly generated. If the PNG is predictable, then an attacker can use that weakness to exploit asymmetric key generation schemes.

Asymmetric public keys should be encapsulated in digital certificates [45]. As discussed in Annex: X.509 Certificate Quick Reference, self-sign is unreliable and represents undue risk without additional security controls. Creating and submitting a Certificate Signing Request [91] to the registration authority (RA) of a CA is part of the key generation stage. The RA authenticates and authorizes the requesting submitter, the CA generates and signs the certificate, and the RA returns it to the requesting entity. If the RA fails to validate the submitter then counterfeit certificates might be issued.

---

* https://cve.mitre.org/cgi-bin/cvename.cgi?name=CVE-2017-15361

Table 7.2   Cryptographic Strengths

Cryptographic Strength	Symmetric Algorithm	Hash Algorithm	ECC Algorithms	RSA/DSA/ DH Algorithms
80-bits	3DES-2K	SHA-1 (160)	160-bits	1024-bits
112-bits	3DES-3K	SHA-2 (224)	224-bits	2048-bits
128-bits	AES-128	SHA-2 (256)	256-bits	3072-bits
192-bits	AES-192	SHA-2 (384)	384-bits	7680-bits
256-bits	AES-256	SHA-2 (512)	512-bits	15360-bits

Worse, if the RA does not operate with appropriate security controls, then counterfeit certificates can be issued, such as the DigiNotor* or Comodo† hacks. Fraudulent code signing certificates were issued, so attackers masqueraded as legitimate software vendors and distribute signed malware posing as trustworthy software.

Key Distribution is necessary when keys are transported from the generation point to the usage point, if they differ. When keys are generated and used within the same device or location, the keys might not need to be distributed. Hence, key distribution is a conditional stage. However, key distribution includes the movement of symmetric, asymmetric private, and asymmetric public keys. When public keys are distributed using legitimate certificates (e.g., CA-signed certificates), the integrity and authenticity has a much higher assurance level. However, symmetric and asymmetric private keys require confidentiality.

Key confidentiality for symmetric and asymmetric private keys is typically done using a KEK that has been previously established. The KEK might be a symmetric key or the recipients' asymmetric public key. The KEK needs to have the equivalent or greater cryptographic strength then the key being exchange, otherwise a weak KEK might compromise the exchanged key. Refer to Table 7.2 for cryptographic strengths. The table is a summary of algorithms and equivalent key lengths from NIST [92]. NIST has calculated the work factor for cryptanalysis using various attacks, but instead of expressing the work in time since that would vary depending on the number and size of computers, the strength is expressed in the number of bits for an exhaustive key search.

For example, 3DES-2K is the triple DES algorithm using two 56-bit keys (encrypt using DES with the first key, decrypt using DES with the second key, and then encrypt using DES with the first key) has 112 key bits but only 80-bit

* www.wired.com/2011/09/diginotar-bankruptcy/
† www.computerworld.com/article/2507509/security0/comodo-hacker-claims-another-certificate-authority.html

strength. However, AES-128 with 128 key bits has 128-bit strength. Conversely, RSA-2048 with 2048 key bits only has 112-bit strength due to various known weaknesses and attacks. Consequently, RSA-2048 is sufficient to encrypt 3DES-2K since they both have 112-bit strength, but it is insufficient to encrypt AES-128. Hence, RSA-3072 should be used for encrypting AES-128 keys. The table only includes the symmetric, asymmetric, and hash algorithms approved by NIST as others have not been publicly evaluated.

For this case study, a payment processor's HSM encountered a hardware failure such that the cryptographic keys were lost. The failover did not happen as expected because the backup HSM had likewise failed months earlier, but the operations team forgot to replace the unit. Backup keys stored in an offsite safe did not help as the hardware chips were empty. The loss of keys resulted in an interruption in payments processing. Consequently, keys from all the banks had to be sent to the payment processor over the weekend and the rush to exchange key components encountered many problems. Keys and key components were faxed as cleartext values, key components were delivered or received by single individuals, and key components were spread over a conference room table accessible by half-a-dozen individuals. The chances of a key compromise were very likely. Whether or not any fraud occurred due to this unpublicized incident is unclear; this particular case study occurred over 20 years ago.

Key Usage occurs after keys are generated and possibly distributed. As discussed in this chapter on Cryptographic Modules, keys might be stored and used in software or hardware. Thus, the protection afforded cryptographic keys varies depending on the cryptographic module security level and the combined application and operational environments. Application and operational controls were discussed in this chapter on Facility Security and System Security. See Figure 7.9 for a graphical interpretation of business security objectives versus security controls. The x-axis represents the four cryptographic module security levels, and the y-axis represents additional security controls provided by the application and operational environments. Theoretically, line of business (LOB) can achieve their security

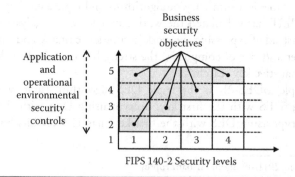

Figure 7.9   Information security levels.

objective using a combination of a cryptographic module with additional application and operational controls.

For this example, five different LOB have approached their security objectives in dissimilar ways. Two businesses have opted for a high (5) security environment, but one has chosen a level 1 cryptographic module, while the other has chosen a level 4 cryptographic module. The former LOB needs to implement strong environmental security controls to compensate for the level 1 module, whereas the latter LOB can rely on the level 4 module with lesser environmental security controls. Conversely, another LOB has likewise chosen a level 1 cryptographic module but with much lower (2) security environment. The other two businesses have chosen medium security environments but with different cryptographic modules: medium (3) with a level 2 module and medium (4) with a level 3 module. Each LOB needs to use its cryptographic keys according to the security policy relative to its cryptographic module and the compensating security controls offered by the various environments.

Another important key usage control is that keys are used for their intended purpose, also called key separation. Key separation goes beyond the cryptographic functions discussed in Chapter 2: encryption, MAC and HMAC, and digital signatures. Rather key usage needs to also address the data types being protected, the application environment, and the business logic being supported. This is best illustrated by examples.

■ Compliant with X9.8 [73], the cardholder PIN is encrypted at the point of entry and remains encrypted during transport to the issuer for verification. While PIN encryption keys (PEKs) might be established using a variety of key management methods as discussed in Chapter 3, a PEK and only a PEK should only be used to protect a PIN. Cryptographic modules are designed to perform PIN translations such that an encrypted PIN is decrypted using one PEK and re-encrypted using another PEK so that the PIN can be sent from one network domain to another without ever being cleartext. However, data encryption keys (DEKs) are intended to encrypt and decrypt other types of data such that cleartext data goes into a cryptographic module and ciphertext comes out, or ciphertext goes in and cleartext goes out. Thus, DEK cannot be used in lieu of PEK because the cleartext PIN would be compromised.

■ Compliant with X9.31 [10], an RSA key pair should not be used for both data encryption and digital signatures. RSA signatures are generated by encrypting a hash using the private key, and verification requires decrypting the hash using the corresponding public key to recover the hash. However, a cryptographic module can be spoofed by submitting ciphertext as a signature; the module will dutifully decrypt the "signature" but instead of returning a decrypted hash, the decrypted ciphertext is revealed. When a relying party encrypts cryptographic material such as a shared secret as is done for TLS, the shared secret is revealed, or when a PIN is encrypted, the PIN is revealed.

Notably, most TLS certificates have both the key encipherment bit for server support and the digital signature bit for client support under the assumption that the TLS software is the sole user.

■ Another example is reusing an RSA key pair originally generated for TLS with password encryption. As noted, most TLS certificates have both the key encipherment bit for server support and the digital signature bit for client support. But TLS certificates typically do not have the data encipherment bit set. Using TLS key pair for passwords violates the certificate key usage bits. Allowing the password process to reuse the TLS keys enables the TLS process to decrypt the password, and the password process to decrypt the TLS shared secret. Thus, both the password and TLS session keys are compromised.

There are so many risks related to reusing keys, it is far easier and better to simply generate separate keys for each specific purpose. Attempting to analyze the various risks and information disclosures for each key reuse case is problematic and time consuming. Subscribing to key separation as a security control is a valid policy and valuable key management practice.

Another important aspect of key usage is key backup and recovery. There are many legitimate scenarios when a cryptographic key is inadvertently lost. Cryptographic modules might suffer a power outage, a catastrophic failure, datacenters might flood, facilities can catch fire, or whole areas might suffer an earthquake. Regardless, copies of keys can be reloaded into recovered or replaced cryptographic hardware or software modules. However, unsafe recovery processes such as the case study described for Key Distribution can significantly increase risk.

Key Revocation is the unexpected termination of a key prior to its expiration. All keys need to have an expiration date; keys cannot be used forever. Probably, the most well-known revocation mechanism is a Certificate Revocation List (CRL) [47], but the Online Certificate Status Protocol (OCSP) [93] is becoming more popular. The CRL is basically a negative list of public key certificates, and by extension the associated private keys, that have been revoked for one reason or another by the issuing CA. OCSP was originally perceived as a positive file of all valid certificates from the issuing CA but has devolved into a negative file, using the CRL as input to maintain the OCSP database. The advantage to a relying party is that a specific certificate can be submitted to an OCSP responder to get its current status. Otherwise, the relying party needs to download the current CRL and check the whole list.

There are no common industry mechanisms for symmetric key revocation. When a symmetric key is revoked, the usual process is to simply change the key. However, it is often the case that new data protected by the new key is insufficient; the old data protected by the old key needs to be considered. For example, when a database encryption key (DBEK) is changed, the data encrypted under the previous DBEK needs to be translated from old to the new DBEK. As another example, if a DEK is changed then any data encrypted under the old DEK might need to be translated to the new DEK or possibly just deleted. Consider a log encryption key (LEK); older logs might be deleted but if the logs need to be retained for a longer period, they might need to be translated to the new LEK. The relative risks of allowing data to be kept encrypted under old keys need to be assessed as revoked keys might still be compromised or determined exhaustively. Copies of older data encrypted using older keys should be migrated to newer keys or deleted altogether.

Some security policies address revocation in the unlikely event of a key compromise; however, there are many legitimate business and operational reasons to prematurely terminate a cryptographic key. For example, when an employee quits or is terminated, any cryptographic keys provisioned by the employer need to be revoked; deactivating employee accounts is necessary but insufficient as keys might be reused by attackers. As another example, TLS keys issued to an online web service need to be revoked when the service is decommissioned. A regrettable scenario is revoking cryptographic keys for deceased customers.

Key Termination is the expected expiration key. As noted, all keys need to have an expiration date; keys cannot be used forever. Unfortunately, it is not uncommon for a security professional to discover keys that have been in use for decades or longer. Probably, the most well-known expiration dates are the not-before and not-after validity dates in digital certificates [13] for the public key; see Annex: X.509 Certificate Quick Reference for an overview of a digital certificate. A common presumption is that the certificate validity dates equally apply to the corresponding private key, but this is not necessarily the case. For example, the public key used to verify a digital signature might have a longer lifecycle than the private key used to generate the digital signature. Case in point, consider a code signing certificate. The signature on the software is often considered valid if the signature date precedes the certificate not-after validity date even after the certificate has expired. The related risk is that the system clock can be adjusted to an earlier time to reflect an earlier software signature.

When symmetric keys or asymmetric private keys expire, the correct practice is to destroy all copies to prevent misuse. Data can no longer be encrypted using an expired key, and data previously encrypted cannot decrypted. Digital signatures can no longer be generated using an expired private key. However, digital signatures might still be verified as every copy of the public key certificate might not be accounted for since certificates are public. The risks related to key termination are overlooking an expired key. Further, there might be business or operational requirements to retain keys past their operational lifecycle when used for authentication and integrity such as MAC, HMAC, or digital signatures.

Key Archive is when keys are retained past their operational lifecycle. Archived keys cannot be allowed to exist in a production environment, otherwise they might be misused. Rather, archived keys are stored in an isolated environment and only used to verify older cryptographically protected data (e.g., HAC, HMAC, digital signatures) for such incidents as fraud investigations, subpoenas, lawsuits, or other legal disputes. Private keys used for digital signatures should never be archived to avoid any possibility of counterfeit signatures. In practice, cryptographic keys are rarely archived. The primary risk related to archiving keys is reinstalling them into production.

7.5 Data Management

Similar to cryptographic keys, data likewise has its own lifecycle. While there are many data management models, Figure 7.10 provides an example state transition diagram for a data lifecycle based on the key management lifecycle discussed in this chapter. The data lifecycle stages are analogous to the key lifecycle stages: (1) data creation, (2) data transfer, (3) data usage with backup and recovery, (4) data deletion, and (4) data retention.

Data creation is when information is first provisioned. For example, an account number is assigned, a password is generated, a social security number is allocated, a name is recorded, an email is typed, a tween is posted, a document is written, or a spreadsheet is saved. Many data elements are created by one organization but shared with many others. For example, when a financial institution creates a credit card primary account number (PAN), the PAN is shared with the cardholder, and the cardholder shares the PAN with hundreds or perhaps thousands of merchants who consequently share the PAN with their payment processor and networks. Thus, one data element created by a single entity might be distributed to thousands of others.

As discussed in Chapter 2, one method of protecting information is tokenization. However, each entity in the work flow must be capable of processing the token versus the original data element. Otherwise, the token must be detokenized.

Data transfer is when information is sent or received. Data encryption over public networks (e.g., Internet), private networks (e.g., Multiprotocol Label Switching or MPLS), or private connections (e.g., leased line) is becoming more common. Encryption solutions such as TLS and IPsec are discussed in Chapter 5, but as discussed in Chapter 3 there are many key management methods available. This chapter also discusses the relative risks of the key management lifecycle that affects cryptography.

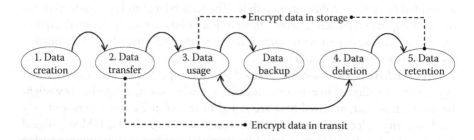

Figure 7.10 Data management lifecycle.

However, another common security controls that need to be considered within the cryptographic architecture is monitoring of encrypted data in transit. Enterprise monitoring was discussed in Chapter 3 and shown again in Figure 7.11 with a browser connecting to a server over TLS. The TLS connection is from the browser, over the Internet, and to the server residing within the DMZ. The server has a TLS asymmetric private and public key pair, and its TLS certificate is shared with the browser. The TLS asymmetric key pair is replicated to a monitoring system residing on the enterprise network. The TLS traffic is captured within the DMZ and likewise replicated to the monitoring system. The monitoring system can replay the TLS handshakes, allowing it to recalculate the session keys, and decrypt traffic.

However, if ephemeral keys are used, the monitoring system cannot recalculate the session keys, as the ephemeral keys lifespan is short and unavailable outside the server. Ephemeral keys were discussed in Chapter 3, and TLS v1.3 was discussed in Chapter 5. TLS v1.3 mandates ephemeral keys for forward secrecy and deprecates RSA for key establishment. Based on current designs, the monitoring system might be unable to relay the TLS handshake; monitoring systems will need to access ephemeral keys.

Another browser-based monitoring method uses MITM certificates, as shown in Figure 7.12. The browser inside the enterprise network connects to a server on the Internet over TLS. However, in this case, the enterprise needs to monitor the inbound traffic for possible malware and outbound traffic for data leakage. The monitoring is done by a proxy server residing in the DMZ which intervenes between the browser and the server; the proxy server is also a certification authority (CA) that issues MITM certificates. MITM certificates work with any TLS cipher suite including ephemeral keys.

The HTTPS call from the browser to the server is redirected to the proxy server which intercepts the server TLS certificate. The proxy CA issues a MITM certificate by duplicating the TLS certificate, replacing the server public key with a proxy

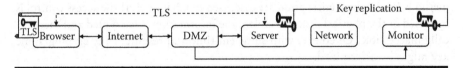

Figure 7.11   Enterprise monitoring.

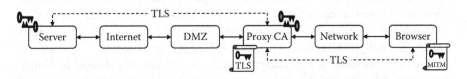

Figure 7.12   MITM monitoring.

public key, and signing the MITM certificate with the proxy CA keys. The browser recognizes the proxy CA and so uses the MITM certificate to establish a TLS connection to the proxy. The proxy uses the TLS certificate to establish a TLS connection to the server. The server assumes the proxy is the browser, so the proxy acts as a TLS client. The browser assumes the proxy is the server, so the proxy also acts as a TLS server. The MITM certificate retains the server subject name so the browser does not incur a name mismatch; however, the server is unaware that a MITM certificate has been issued in its name with a forged public key.

Data usage is when information is stored and subsequently read or written. Read access and write access are fundamental access control mechanisms. Logical access controls for networks, systems, applications, databases, and other nonvolatile storage devices restrict data access to authorized users and administrators. However, if an access control can be bypassed or deceived then information might be disclosed to unauthorized attackers. Bypassing includes physical access to storage devices, which avoids network controls. Local console access might circumvent system, application, or database access controls. Identity theft, stealing passwords, fake credentials, social engineering, and hacking systems can deceive access controls. Consequently, data monitoring and database encryption have evolved as information security controls.

Data monitoring observes information objects at the system, file, record, or field level for various types of access. Monitoring tools typically do not authenticate nor authorize access, rather they compare actions against security policy. For example, if an individual has read-only access, but an administrator enables write access, the monitoring system would trigger an alert. As another example, if a database is accessed by an unexpected protocol or port that violates a security policy, the monitor system triggers another alert.

Database encryption keeps information encrypted on disk and only decrypts information in memory when needed. Encryption might be managed at the database table, database column, system file, record, or field level. Key management methods for database encryption are discussed in Chapter 3. If the access control is bypassed or the physical disks are stolen, the information is encrypted and theoretically inaccessible. Of course, with sufficient time and resources any cryptographic key might be determined.

Data deletion is when information is erased from storage. However, unlike a cryptographic key where all instances are destroyed, data deletion might occur in stages. Information aged on one system might not have the same expiration on another. Backup copies are sometimes kept as part of data retention. Another consideration is when information is in the cloud. Third-party data deletion is often very difficult to manage, verify, and audit. Often third-party service providers including cloud providers do not permit audits of storage systems.

Another misnomer is that encrypted data can be logically deleted by simply destroying the cryptographic key; however, this is no longer the case. As noted with data usage, given sufficient time and resources, any cryptographic key might be determined. An exhaustive key attack is always viable if the data holds its value past the time it takes to determine the key.

Data retention is for long-term information storage. As noted in data deletion, backup copies are sometimes kept for data retention. Data retention varies by industry such as health care versus financial services, by business such as automobile loans versus mortgages, or by company policy. However, if the retention period exceeds the key lifecycle, the cryptography needs to be transitioned [94] possibly from one key to another, a longer key size, or even another algorithm.

For example, a document signed with an RSA 512-bit key in 1980 would be insecure in 1990, and an RSA 1024-bit key in 1990 is considered insecure in 2010. The proper method to preserve the chain of evidence is to preserve each signature by re-signing the signed document as demonstrated in Figure 7.13. The original document signed with an RSA-512 key is signed with an RSA-1024 key, again with an RSA-2048 key, and eventually signed with an ECDSA-256 key. Note that the hash sizes also need to increase. Each signature needs to include the digital signature algorithm, the hash algorithm, and the public key certificate [95].

For another example, a document encrypted using DES in 1980 would be insecure in 2000, and the same document encrypted using 2K-3DES in 2000 would be insecure in 2010. Likewise, the document encrypted using AES-128 in 2010 might be at risk in 2030 if quantum computer become operational. The data might be decrypted and re-encrypted for each key and algorithm; however, the proper method to preserve the chain of evidence is to preserve each encryption as shown in Figure 7.14. The original document encrypted using DES is doubly encrypted using 2K-3DES, and then again using 3K-3DES, then AES-128, and eventually using AES-256. Each encrypted layer needs to indicate the algorithm and symmetric key [95].

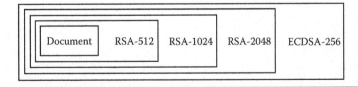

Figure 7.13   Signature transitions.

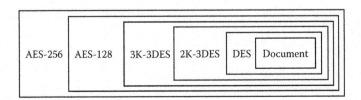

Figure 7.14   Encryption transitions.

The data management lifecycle differs from the key management lifecycle in stages and lifetimes, so the cryptographic transitions need to be managed. From a cryptographic architecture perspective, the relative risks include data disclosure for confidentiality, data modification or substitution for authentication and integrity, and deniability for non-repudiation. Data stored in one decade is susceptible to more powerful computers or mathematical advances in the next decade. For example, information encrypted today might be vulnerable to quantum computers by the next decade, including copies of the ciphertext stored in unforeseen locations such as cloud storage or perhaps attackers planning for long-term fraud.

Chapter 8

Security Assessments

The role of a security professional includes information security consulting. Consulting includes determining what security controls are in place, identifying control gaps, assisting lines of business (LOB) in assessing risks, and recommending solutions. However, determining controls can often be problematic. As discussed in Chapter 1, knowledge is often dispersed among various teams such as application groups, network group, database group, administrators, and various developers. Collecting and consolidating information is an important skill for any security professional; as shown in Figure 8.1, this includes sifting through documentation, conducting interviews, testing, performing analysis, and eventually producing reports.

At the initiation of the assessment, the security professional might have little to no information regarding the problems, products, applications, environments, or the business. Gathering information can often be difficult. The assessor might be external to the enterprise for an independent assessment or an employee for an internal evaluation. The size, complexity, and organizational structure of the enterprise can impede knowledge sharing. Individuals or groups might withhold pertinent information due to internal politics, personal agendas, or denial of responsibilities. Product manufacturers and service providers are sometimes reluctant to share details or unable due to knowledge loss. Mergers, acquisitions, end of product lifecycles, and rebranding can affect information. Donald Rumsfeld was quoted [96] describing the known and the unknown conditions in his report to the North Atlantic Treaty Organization in 2002.

> Now what is the message there? The message is that there are no "knowns." There are things we know that we know. There are known unknowns. That is to say there are things that we now know we don't know. But there are also unknown unknowns. There are things we

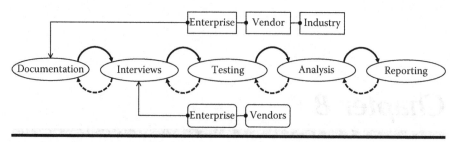

Figure 8.1 Assessment process.

don't know we don't know. So when we do the best we can and we pull all this information together, and we then say well that's basically what we see as the situation, that is really only the known knowns and the known unknowns. And each year, we discover a few more of those unknown unknowns.

Donald Rumsfeld

Assessments have similar problems. With regard to cryptography, there are known knowns, misunderstood knowns (things to be true but are actually false), known unknowns, and of course unknown unknowns. There is also information, misinformation (false or incorrect information), and even disinformation (false information spread deliberately to deceive). Some engagements might be antagonistic in nature, one or more of the groups might not want the assessment, while others may welcome the evaluation. The assessor must work through all of these hurdles to determine when sufficient information has been gathered via documentation, interviews, and testing to perform analysis and develop the report.

8.1 Documentation

Documentation is the cornerstone of any assessment. While hallway conversations, emails, chat sessions, and phone calls are all acceptable methods to gather information, at the end of the day only official documentation is reliable. Basically, if it is not documented it does not exist. Official documentation should be on company letterhead or equivalent stationary. Enterprise policy, standards, practices, and procedures need to be documented. Vendor services, product manuals, user guidelines, and technical specifications need to be documented. Refer to Figure 8.1 for an overview of documentation inputs.

Prior to exchanging any documents, conducting any interviews, or performing any tests, a kickoff meeting should be held to discuss the engagement scope, expectations, timeline, LOB, resources, applications, products, and vendors. Resources include available and needed documentation, contact information, list of interviewees, and relevant environments including production and test systems.

Ideally, all relevant documentation is provided to the assessor prior to scheduling any interviews or scheduling any tests. The assessor needs sufficient time to review the documentation in preparation for interviews, otherwise info provided by interviewees is uncorroborated. Likewise, the assessor needs adequate time to read the documentation as background material for planning test cases with expected results. Depending on the volume of documentation, days or weeks might be needed to sift through all the material. Enterprise documentation might include policy, standards, practices, or procedures.

- **Enterprise security policies** typically define high-level responsibilities (the "who") and requirements (the "what"). Responsibilities can be defined at the senior management level, identifying which organizational groups are accountable. Requirements might be broadly outlined and refer to various regulatory, legal, and industry organizations.

- **Enterprise security standards** usually define medium-level responsibilities (the "who") and requirements (the "what"), characteristically expanding on the security policy, and sometimes provide high-level "how" specifications. Responsibilities might identify which managerial teams are accountable. Requirements are more explicit and refer to exact regulations, laws, and industry standards.

- **Enterprise security practices** typically define low-level specifications (the "how") and justifications (the "why"), often organized by the security standards. Practices specify products, tools, resources, and named procedures. For example, certificate policy and certificate practice statement documents are integral components for operating a certification authority. Justifications identify relative risks and related countermeasures provided by the security practices.

- **Enterprise security procedures** provide detailed instructions (the "how"), sometimes locational information (the "where"), and specific roles (the "who"). Procedures are step-by-step tasks executed using products and tools at designated locations per role assignment (e.g., security officer). Executing procedures typically includes capturing sign-in sheets, checklists, and various system and application logs.

An external assessor would likely be unfamiliar with enterprise documentation, and thus might need more time to read the material. However, while policy might be shared publicly, the more detailed standards, practices and especially procedures need to be protected, which is often done under a nondisclosure agreement (NDA). Conversely, an internal assessor would be familiar with most of the enterprise documentation, and no NDA is needed for employees, but time is still needed to review the various documents. Only relevant enterprise documentation needs to be read or reviewed, but determining which documents are pertinent can be problematic. The kickoff meeting enables discussion for determining enterprise documentation and vendor documentation which might include service or product manuals, user guidelines, technical specifications, or white papers.

- **Service Manuals** present a high-level overview of available applications offered by the third-party providers. While few technical details are included, important information includes service names, acronyms, abbreviations, and vendor website.
- **Product Manuals** provide a high-level overview of available applications offered by the software manufacturer. While few technical details are included, important information includes product names, acronyms, abbreviations, and vendor website.

An important issue regarding vendor information is accuracy. Often application teams refer to products by the vendor name and not the service or product name. Further, service and product names can change due to marketing, but teams might refer to the older names. Also, mergers and acquisition can change the company name, end product lines, and begin new ones. Any of these factors create confusion which the security professional needs to decipher.

- **User Guidelines** provide great detail on how to install, configure, register, and employ services or products, but screenshots convey few technical details. The assessor often needs to "read between the lines" to acquire specifics. For example, a complete list of cryptographic algorithms might be discovered from a graphic pull-down menu.
- **Technical Specifications** can offer the details needed by an assessor but too frequently such documentation is unavailable. Vendors might not document such information for a variety of reasons. Services or products might change frequently enough such that details are not fully documented. Some vendors prefer to not document technical details and keep such knowledge verbally. Other vendors might have lost knowledge due to reliance on contractors, use of cryptographic libraries, or employee attrition. Yet other vendors refuse to share technical specifications regardless of any agreements.
- **White Papers** written by vendors might provide some technical details. Not all vendors publish white papers. More often marketing papers discussing the advantages of the vendor's services or products are available. Marketing papers rarely offer any significant technical information. Further, they tend to misuse terminology or generalize claims such that it is sometimes better to skip marketing papers.

With regard to vendor documentation, information gathered as hearsay is unsubstantiated and hence unreliable. Essentially, if it is undocumented it does not exist.

Further, if it is not from an authoritative source even the documentation is questionable. Vendor interviews help corroborate vendor-provided documentation, but vendor-related documentation from an independent source is preferable. For example, as discussed in Chapter 7, many products are evaluated per the National Institute of Standards and Technology (NIST) cryptographic algorithm validation program (CAVP) and cryptographic module validation program (CMVP). The corresponding security policy listing both Federal Information Processing Standard (FIPS) and non-FIPS algorithms and key lengths has been verified by an NIST-accredited laboratory which represents an independent and authoritative evaluation. While there are several evaluation programs available worldwide, all are based on various industry standards. The importance of industry standards is paramount. Industry documentation might include standards, specifications, guidelines, research papers, articles, or press releases.

- **Industry standards** cover a wide range of topics, including cryptographic algorithms, key management schemes, security protocols as discussed in Chapters 4 and 5, and inform security management policy and practices. Conventional standards language defines requirements using "shall" or "must" statements, recommendations as "should" sentences, and options as "may" observations. Standards organizations were described in Chapter 1.
- **Industry specifications** address a broad range of security protocols. Whereas standards focus on "what" and "why" alternatively specification address "how" things are done, more so for interoperability. However, specification often uses similar "shall" and "should" language. Vendor services and products might implement an industry specification by developing software often based on cryptographic libraries, or incorporate an existing cryptographic tool. However, as discussed in Chapter 7, there is often a gap between implementation versus specification.
- **Industry guidelines** provide advice and information on implementing standards and specifications. Guidelines have many alternate names including technical report, supplemental, recommendation, and the like. While guidelines do not have the same status as standards or specifications, they can provide relevant information regarding recent vulnerabilities or configuration advice. Guidance can originate from any source such as standards organizations, regulatory agencies, universities, and even vendors.
- **Industry research papers** can provide details regarding Common Vulnerabilities and Exposures[*] (CVE) for algorithms, protocols, crypto libraries, or products. Sometimes the research paper is publicly available or it might have limited distribution, but the CVE is typically posted. Applications, products, or services susceptible to known vulnerabilities which need to be fixed. Unfortunately, zero-day attacks are problematic.

---

[*] https://cve.mitre.org/

- **Industry articles** provide current news regarding data breaches, threats, hacks, and newly posted CVE. Articles can also offer opinion pieces regarding product safety, reliability, and efficiency. Some articles provide links to other articles, industry research papers, or websites with related information.
- **Industry press releases** provide current news regarding mergers, acquisitions, divestitures, bankruptcy, and other announcements. Press releases can help clarify vendor names, product names, product releases, and even acronyms.

Enterprise, vendor, and industry documentation can establish a foundational knowledge base for any assessment. Undocumented information is fundamentally unreliable information. A kickoff meeting to discuss documentation among other project issues is helpful. The assessor needs time to review documentation prior to interviews or testing. Unfortunately, documentation is often unavailable or provided by request during the initial interviews.

8.2 Interviews

Interviews are a crucial assessment mechanism to corroborate documentation. Refer to Figure 8.1 for an overview of interview inputs. Interviews include conversations within the enterprise and with vendors. Enterprise interviews are with business managers, application managers, database managers, administrators, engineers, developers, and possibly contractors. Vendor interviews might be with account representatives, product managers, or engineers.

Some assessments might be adversarial in nature. For example, an external assessor might be assigned by another legal authority for a necessary but unwelcomed assessment. As another example, an external or internal assessor might be assigned by an internal authoritative group such as senior management or internal audit. Conversely, a more cooperative assessment is when the project team requests an assessment to engage a security professional.

When documentation is previously available, it can be used to coordinate interviews versus haphazardly discussing topics or asking random questions. Documentation should be listed in order of priority, and then the various table of contents can be used as an agenda. Care should be taken to avoid repeatedly asking the same question. However, at the same time, the same topic can be queried to confirm answers. As questions are asked and answers are collected, it is extremely important to be mindful for conflicting or inconsistent answers. This is especially true tracking answers from one interview to another.

Inconsistent or conflictual answers can occur for a variety of reasons. The interviewee might inadvertently have misinformation. Alternatively, the interviewee might intentionally provide disinformation. Another possibility is that the actual processes do not comply with the documented policy, practices, or procedures. It is not uncommon to discover any of the following: obviously, the fourth scenario is the best situation.

1. Processes are inconsistent and undocumented.
2. Processes are consistent but undocumented.
3. Processes are consistent and documented but not always followed.
4. Processes are consistent, documented, and followed.

When documentation is not previously available, questions can be queued up and submitted to interviewees ahead of time to allow preparing answers. However, without reliable information on which to base questions, such inquires tend to be generic in nature. Again, any answers provided by a vendor might need to be protected, which is often done under an NDA. Documentation can be requested during these types of interviews.

Even when documents are previously available, the interview will likely uncover some other documentation not provided. Thus, as indicated by the dotted line in Figure 8.1, the assessor should expect to ask for additional documents. Naturally, additional documents may lead to additional interviews. The documentation versus interview cycle is sometimes considered to be a never-ending cycle; however, eventually the assessor will reach a point of diminishing returns where no substantive information is uncovered. There are two basic results: either no further information is available and things look good, or things look so bad that no further interviews (or documentation) will make things better.

During the interview, notes are taken. The notes should be typed up and shared, and if more than one person is taking notes, they should be consolidated. Any differences need to be reconciled with the interviewee. However, follow-up interviews are not always needed, simple or easy questions might be handled by email, phone, text, or other method. But, all answers need to be documented. The notes are updated, accordingly with a version number or date to indicate changes. Differences exposed between the documentation and interviewee should be addressed during the interview. If the issue cannot be resolved during the interview, then it should be added to an issue list for reconciliation.

An issues list is maintained and updated across all the interviews. As each issue is resolved, the list is updated and cross-referenced to the notes. Some issues might be determined irrelevant and can be resolved, while others might be overtaken by events (OBE). For example, an OBE might be a bug with older software version that has since been fixed. An irrelevant issue might be an erroneous process that has no security affect. The issues list and notes might be managed in the same or separate document.

The notes include date and time, the meeting venue such as conference call or location of the face-to-face meeting, a list of attendees, interviewers, interviewees, questions, answers, issues, and list of relevant documentation. Resolutions are cross-referenced to the issues list. The notes and issues list might be managed in the same or separate document.

During the interview, an interviewer leads the discussion. Too many participants attempting to interact with the interviewee is chaos. Interviews might be conducted by a small team of interviewers, but one person must take the lead. A single interviewee is preferable, but often small teams are assembled to cover topics. Similarly, one person must take the interviewee lead, directing questions to the appropriate person. Further, interviews often have observers, but again one person must be the lead interviewer. Regardless, too many participants increase distractions, whether it be background noise, side conversations, or interruptions. Participation should be kept to a minimum to reduce complications.

8.3 Testing

Testing can be an important assessment technique to validate normal processing or security controls when normal processing does not trigger an incident. For a normal processing example, consider when a password needs to be reset due to a forgetful user. Testing can be accomplished by a user accessing the password reset page and following the directions. A temporary password sent to the user via email is used for logon to the system. Each normal test case also needs to be well defined. The configuration parameters need to be established, the expected result needs to be documented, the actual results need to be recorded, and evidence needs to be captured. For example, test case #12 is testing password reset (Table 8.1).

For an incident example, consider when a user enters the correct password and the system allows access. Alternatively, procedures addressing the number of logon attempts and temporary password time-outs do not occur during normal processing. Testing can be arranged for each exception: exceed the number of logon attempts, and attempt using a temporary password after it has expired. Each test will have an expected result that can be verified; screenshots or security logs might be captured as evidence. When an unexpected test result is observed, it is possible the test configuration is invalid, the test is invalid, the control is in error, or sometimes the control itself is invalid.

Table 8.1   Test Case: Password Reset

Test Case #12 Password Reset

1. Access the password reset page and click on password reset linka
    a. Enter user name (Sam Test) and email address (sam.test@example.com)
    b. Verify system log and timestamp

2. Open email message with temporary password   a. Verify email message timestamp
3. Logon with user name (Sam Test) and temporary password   a. Verify system access and timestamp

- If the test configuration is invalid, the configuration needs to be revised, and the test needs to be repeated.
- If the test is invalid, the control needs to be reviewed, the test configuration needs to be revised, and the test needs to be repeated.
- If the control is in error, either the control needs to be remediated or the documentation needs to be revised.

Upon occasion, the control itself might be invalid. The application or system might not be able to detect the incident or be unable to protect against its occurring. For example, a policy might state that employees never write down passwords. However, there is no technical control to enforce such a policy. No hardware or software control can feasibly ascertain whether an employee has written a password on a piece of paper. The policy might be valid and procedural controls might enforce the policy, such as a statement in an employee handbook and mandatory training, but no technical control can be tested.

Each incident test case also needs to be well defined. Likewise the configuration parameters need to be established, the expected result needs to be documented, the actual results need to be recorded, and evidence needs to be captured. For example, test case #13 is testing the number of logon attempts, and test case #14 is testing temporary password time-outs (Tables 8.2 and 8.3).

The system logs and email need to be captured as evidence. Screenshots might also be captured. Once testing is completed, the test account needs to be deactivated. Hence, every test case will have pre-execution, execution, and post-execution tasks. As the test cases are completed, issues might arise that require follow-up interviews or additional documentation, as indicated by the dotted lines in Figure 8.1. However, as discussed earlier follow-up interviews are not always needed, simple or easy questions might be handled by email, phone, text, or other method. Further, the documentation versus interview cycle, and the interview versus test cycle will eventually reach a point of diminishing returns. But, all answers

Table 8.2   Test Case: Logon Attempts

Test Case #13 Exceed Number of Logon Attempts
1. Allocate test account with user name (Sam Test) and password (Test1234)

2. Attempt first logon with user name (Sam Test) and password (Test1111)
  a. Warning message: logon failed, attempt 1 of 3
  b. Verify system log and timestamp

3. Attempt second logon with user name (Sam Test) and password (Test2222)
  a. Warning message: logon failed, attempt 2 of 3
  b. Verify system log and timestamp

4. Attempt third logon with user name (Sam Test) and password (Test3333)
  a. Warning message: logon failed attempt 3 of 3 – click on password reset link
  b. Verify system log and timestamp

Table 8.3 Test Case: Temporary Password

Test Case #14 Exceed Temporary Password Time-out

1. Click on password reset link
  a. Enter user name (Sam Test) and email address (sam.test@example.com)
  b. Verify system log and timestamp

2. Open email message with temporary password
  a. Verify email message states password expires in 15 minutes
  b. Verify email message timestamp
  c. Wait 15 minutes and 5 seconds for temporary password to expire

3. Attempt logon with user name (Sam Test) and temporary password
  a. Warning message: logon failed attempt 1 of 1 – click on password reset link
  b. Verify system log and timestamp

need to be documented. Ultimately, the test cases and results along with interview notes and documentation are input to the analysis phase.

8.4 Analysis

Analysis is an essential process of the assessment as it is the culmination of documentation, interview notes, and testing results. Figure 8.1 shows analysis logically occurring sequentially after documentation, interviews, and testing; however, analysis actually begins at or about documentation reviews and continues into reporting. Analysis ends when sufficient information has been confirmed to determine the cryptographic architecture.

The process of analysis is actually rather straightforward. Facts are compiled and crossed referenced to documentation, interviews, and testing. Each fact might have multiple references, and some facts might have several references in common (Table 8.4). Consistencies are noted, but inconsistencies need to be resolved. For example, if the documentation provides a list of cryptographic algorithms, but interviews reveal a different list, and testing cannot corroborate the differences, the issues need to be resolved.

Table 8.4 provides an example analysis worksheet with four fact statements, scores, and references. The scores are rated from 0 to 10 with 10 the best and 0 the worst. The references in the worksheet are cross-referenced with those in the reference list.

■ Fact #1 identifies that the product "X" has FIPS 140-2 certification with a best score of 10, and four references: the product technical specification, the NIST certificate, the corresponding FIPS 140-2 security policy, and notes from interview #1. The technical specification refers to the FIPS 140-2

Table 8.4 Analysis Worksheet

Facts	Scores	References
1. Product X has FIPS 140-2 certification	10	a. Product X technical specification[1] b. NIST certificate #nnnn[2] c. Security policy #nnnn[3] d. Interview #1 on mm/dd/yyyy[4]
2. Product X supports AES-256 and AES-128	10	a. Product X technical specification[1] b. Security policy #nnnn[3] c. Interview #2 on mm/dd/yyyy[5]
3. Product X supports 2K, and 3K 3DES	6	a. Product X technical specification[1] b. Security policy #nnnn[3] c. Interview #2 on mm/dd/yyyy[4]
4. Product X supports DES 56-bit and exportable DES 40-bit	2	a. Security policy #nnnn[3] b. Interview #2 on mm/dd/yyyy[4]

[1] Product X technical specification.
[2] NIST certificate #nnnn.
[3] Security policy #nnnn.
[4] Interview #1 on mm/dd/yyyy.
[5] Interview #2 on mm/dd/yyyy.

certification, and the certificate number was provided in the interview. The assessor was able to look up the certificate and the corresponding security policy.

■ Fact #2 states that the product supports the advanced encryption standard (AES) algorithm with another score of 10 and three references: the technical specification, the NIST FIPS 140-2 security policy, and notes from interview #2. The first interviewee could only corroborate the NIST certificate but could not provide details regarding algorithms. The NIST certificate provides general vendor and product information, but the corresponding security plan lists the FIPS and non-FIPS algorithms. The second interviewee was able to verify the AES algorithms.

■ Fact #3 refers to the two-key (2K) and three-key (3K) triple-DES (2DES) algorithm, with a lower score of 6 because of its lesser key length and cryptographic strengths, with the same three references as AES. The second interviewee was able to verify the 3DES algorithms.

■ Fact #4 refers to the DES algorithm and the exportable DES key length, with the lower score of 2 and two references: the NIST FIPS 140-2 security policy, and notes from interview #2. The technical specification neglected to mention the DES algorithm, but the security plan did not. The second interviewee was able to verify the DES algorithms.

Thus, as the analysis is performed, concerns might arise that require follow-up testing, interviews, or additional documentation, as indicated by the dotted lines in Figure 8.1. However, the documentation versus interview cycle, the interview versus test cycle, and the test versus analysis cycle will eventually reach a point of diminishing returns. The ability to determine when to pursue an issue and at what time to discontinue investigation is part of the skill set of a good assessor. William James (1842–1910), an American philosopher and psychologist, once observed [97] that differences are sometimes insignificant:

> A difference which makes no difference is no difference at all.

> **William James**

The assessor needs to recognize when an issue becomes immaterial. If one or more issues represent equivalent risk then further research is irrelevant. For example, the original single DES algorithm employs a 56-bit key which by current standards is too weak, and pre-1992 restricted exportable DES to a 40-bit key. However, some cryptographic modules retain DES (56-bits) and exportable DES (40-bits) for backward compatibility. Since any use of DES is an unacceptable risk, the details regarding anything weaker than DES is immaterial although the risks are relevant and need to be factored into the analysis and summarized into the report.

Some facts are positive while others are negative. For example, a cryptographic module certified per the NIST cryptographic algorithm (CAVP) and cryptographic module (CMVP) validation programs is a positive fact. Further, the list of FIPS-approved algorithms in the security policy is another positive fact. Conversely, the list of non-FIPS algorithm might be a negative. And if the list of non-FIPS algorithms includes DES and exportable DES, then these would definitely be negative facts. Suspicions or unsubstantiated opinions are not facts; they cannot be treated as such and should not be represented in the report.

The analysis process can be arduous and is typically done using spreadsheets or online tools; but for smaller engagements, the draft reports might be used. For each factoid, a numeric score should be assigned and the associated justification is referenced. The score reflects the advantages versus the disadvantages using a range of values (e.g., using a scale of 1–10 where 10 is best and 0 is worst). Additionally, version control and track changes are paramount. When more than one assessor is involved, as is common with larger projects, keeping track of action items, edits, and updates is critical. Further, the assessors' unedited notes and any intermediate drafts should not be shared to manage expectations.

8.5 Reporting

Reporting is the culmination of reviewing documentation, conducting interviews, executing tests, and performing analysis. The enterprise might provide a template to the assessor, regardless of whether the assessor is external or internal, and insist it to be used. Alternatively, the enterprise might provide a template as an example that the assessor is expected to customize. Otherwise, the enterprise might expect the assessor to provide a report format. Regardless, the report needs to reflect the facts determined during the analysis phase (Table 8.5).

The sample report is organized in four sections: executive summary, report summary, report details, and report references. Its structure is based on the premise that an advantage or disadvantage can be rated as significant, important, or meaningful. More or fewer ratings are possible, but three are used for this example. The numerical scoring used in the analysis can be and should be used to determine the verbal rating in the report.

- Significant advantages are those that provide the best security controls. For example, current algorithms with larger keys (e.g., AES-256) is stronger than shorter keys or older algorithms (e.g., 3DES).
- Important advantages are those that provide better security controls. For example, current algorithms with shorter keys (e.g., AES-128) is better than older algorithms (e.g., 2K-DES or 3K-DES).
- Meaningful advantages are those that provide good security controls. For example, older algorithms (e.g., 3K-DES) are acceptable than deprecated algorithms (e.g., DES).

Table 8.5   Example Security Assessment Report

Security Assessment Report on Product X
1. Executive Summary 1.1. Significant advantages 1.2. Significant disadvantages 1.3. Significant recommendations
2. Report Summary 2.1. List of significant and important advantages 2.2. List of significant and important disadvantages 2.3. List of significant and important recommendations
3. Report Details 3.1. Discussion on advantages with cross-references 3.2. Discussion on disadvantages with cross-references 3.3. Discussion of associated recommendations
4. Report References 4.1. List of documentation 4.2. List of interviews 4.3. List of test cases

■ Significant disadvantages are those that are the worst vulnerabilities. For example, storing or transmitting cleartext sensitive data.

■ Important disadvantages are those that are worse vulnerabilities. For example, using older cryptographic software with known bugs.

■ Meaningful disadvantages are those that are bad vulnerabilities. For example, using deprecated algorithms (e.g., DES).

The executive summary includes the significant advantages and disadvantages along with any associated recommendations. Executive summaries are optional and not always needed, but some enterprise prefer them. When an executive summary is included, it is common to only address the more significant issues. However, identifying significant disadvantages without providing recommendations is an incomplete report. Disadvantages should either be remediated by fixes or enhancements, or alternatively by compensating controls. Compensating controls are additional constraints that can be applied to the existing product under assessment. For example, if a product uses a vulnerable protocol over a port address, and the protocol cannot be disabled within the product, the port address might be blocked to prevent access to the protocol. The executive summary should include a final accept or reject status. Note that the acceptance might be conditional based on the recommendations.

The report summary includes the significant advantages and disadvantages along with the important advantages and disadvantages. If an executive summary is not included, then the significant advantages and disadvantages are fully spelled out in the report summary; however, if an executive summary is included then an abridged version of the significant advantages and disadvantages might be used in the report summary with a cross-reference to the executive summary. Regardless, a discussion of the recommendations for the significant and important disadvantages is included in the report summary. If no executive summary is provided, then the report summary should include a final accept or reject status. Note that acceptance might be conditional based on the recommendations.

The report details include all of the significant, important, and meaningful items for the advantages and disadvantages. Each item is cross-referenced to the various documents, interviews, and test cases. Further, the report details address all of the associated recommendations for reconciling the disadvantages. It is likely that few recipients will read the whole report; often only the summaries are reviewed. Items considered immaterial and sufficiently inconsequential to not be rated as meaningful can be disregarded in the report. The analysis worksheet will include all of the issues and can always be examined.

The report references list the documentation, interviews, and test cases. The documentation lists include the enterprise, vendor, and industry documents. Regular references include the document name, authors (if applicable), source, and date. The interview list should include the date, attendees, associations (e.g., company name, title), and topic. The test cases should include a test case name, reference number, and date. In addition to the reference list, reports might include one or more appendices to provide further details. Supplemental information might be provided by separate presentation material.

Chapter 9

Illustrations

9.1 Hypothetical Mobile Transaction

Figure 9.1 shows an example architecture for handling mobile transactions. Reading the diagram from left to right, a mobile store (mStore) provisions a mobile device. The mobile device connects to the web server and sends a message. The web server connects to the app server and forwards the message for processing. The app server connects to the database (DB) server to fetch the device profile. The DB server connects to the key management (KM) server for DB encryption keys.

Each entity within the example mobile architecture uses cryptographic keys for a variety of purposes including Transport Layer Security (TLS), Secure Shell (SSH), database encryption (DBE), and mobile security. The following cryptographic keys are deployed within the mobile environment.

- The mStore generates a unique asymmetric key pair per mobile device. The public key is encapsulated in an X.509 digital certificate issued by an external (commercial) certification authority (CA_1). The private key and the complete certificate chain is installed onto the mobile device for TLS connections.
- The mobile device, in addition to its TLS private key and certificate chain, might use one or more unique symmetric keys for a variety of reasons. For example, a symmetric might be used to encrypt the asymmetric private key, authentication data (e.g., password), or other sensitive data (e.g., account number). White-box cryptography might be used to obfuscate the symmetric key; various key bits are scattered throughout the mobile device using a pseudo-random pattern known only to the mobile device. The mobile application might be further obfuscated by rearranging executable code such that each mobile device has a relatively unique software version, making reverse engineering difficult.

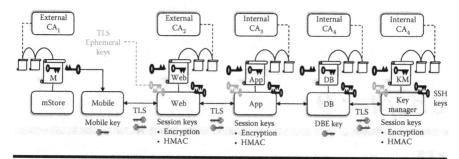

Figure 9.1   Example mobile transaction.

■ The web server has its own TLS private key and certificate chain, the certificates issued by a different external (commercial) CA_2. In addition to the TLS static keys, the web server might also employ ephemeral keys. The TLS handshake negotiates the session unique symmetric encryption and Hash Message Authentication Code (HMAC) keys with the mobile device. A successful TLS handshake requires that the web server recognizes the CA_1 certificate chain and the mobile device recognizes the CA_2 certificate chain. The web server also has asymmetric SSH keys for key agreement to negotiate session symmetric encryption keys and for digital signature authentication with administrators.

■ The app server has its own TLS private key and certificate chain, the certificates issued by an internal (private) CA_3. In addition to the TLS static keys, the web server might also employ ephemeral keys. The TLS handshake negotiates the session unique symmetric encryption and HMAC keys with the web server. A successful TLS handshake requires that the app server recognizes the CA_2 certificate chain and the web server recognizes the CA_3 certificate chain. The app server also has asymmetric SSH keys for key agreement to negotiate session symmetric encryption keys and for digital signature authentication with administrators.

■ The DB server has its own TLS private key and certificate chain, the certificates issued by an internal (private) CA_4 same as the KM server. In addition to the TLS static keys, the DB server also has DBE keys managed by the KM server. The DB server also has asymmetric SSH keys for key agreement to negotiate session symmetric encryption keys and for digital signature authentication with administrators.

■ The KM server has its own TLS private key and certificate chain, the certificates issued by an internal (private) CA_4. In addition to the TLS static keys, the KM server might also employ ephemeral keys. The TLS handshake negotiates the session unique symmetric encryption and HMAC keys with the DB server. A successful TLS handshake requires that the DB server recognizes the CA_4 certificate chain and the KM server recognizes the CA_4 certificate chain. The KM server also has asymmetric SSH keys for key agreement to negotiate session symmetric encryption keys and for digital signature authentication with administrators.

Some keys are managed by external parties. For example, the mStore is an external party to the organization, as is essentially the mobile device. The cryptographic keys generated by the mStore and installed into mobile devices are basically beyond the control of the organization without any legal or other contractual obligations. Further, the certificates used by the mobile device are issued by CA_1 which is another external party. Also, the certificates used by the web app are issued by CA_2 another external party. The web app uses commercially issued certificates recognizable by the mobile device; a mobile device would not necessarily be able to trust certificates from a private CA (e.g., CA_3 or CA_4).

Different groups within the same organization might managed dissimilar keys. For example, the two internal certificate authorities (e.g., CA_3 and CA_4) might be managed by an enterprise public key infrastructure (PKI) group. Alternatively, the two certificate authorities might be managed by different groups; the internal CA_3 might be managed by the enterprise PKI group, whereas CA_4 might be specific to the KM servers operated by another group. The SSH administrator keys might be managed by another group altogether, such as system administrators. The DBE keys might be managed by DB administrators. Thus, multiple groups might be managing various keys throughout the organization, but hopefully compliant to enterprise policy and standards.

9.2 EMV Payment Cards

EMV® is an abbreviation for three card payment brands: EuroPay, MasterCard, and Visa (EMV) covering various payment technologies. Mastercard integrated with Europay* International in 2002 to become a private share corporation, but the name EMV and the company EMVCo† continues its operations. EMV® technologies cover a variety of payment-related methods including integrated circuit chip (ICC) contact and contactless specifications, its mobile specifications, token payment specifications, quick response two-dimensional specifications, and its three-domain (3-D) secure specification.

The EMV smartcard (ICC) payment card is an alternative to the legacy magnetic stripe (magstripe) payment cards. EMV payment "chip and PIN" card specifications were available as early as 1994, but worldwide adoption was slow for several reasons. First, there was no smartcard infrastructure; point-of-sale (POS) terminals and automated teller machines (ATMs) only had magstripe readers. Second, the

---

* https://www.mastercard.us/en-us/about-mastercard/who-we-are/history.html
† https://www.emvco.com/

costs associated with replacing legacy POS, ATM, and magstripe cards was another hurdle that had to be overcome. Consequently, hybrid cards with both legacy magstripe and ICC have been issued. Figure 9.2 demonstrates the security and cryptography [98] for a hybrid payment card ecosystem consisting of the issuer, cardholder, merchant, acquirer, and network.

The issuer, typically a financial institution, sends a payment card to the cardholder. The cardholder uses the card with PIN at a merchant location. For online authorization, the merchant sends an authorization request message to the acquirer, the merchant's financial institution. The acquirer forwards the request to the payment network. The network routes the request to the issuer. The issuer checks the cardholder profile, and returns an authorization response message to the network, acquirer, and merchant. Online PIN verification undergoes the following steps.

1. The issuer creates a PIN using the PIN verification key (PVK) and sends a PIN mailer to the cardholder. The PIN mailer contains the cleartext PIN so the cardholder can memorize the PIN.
2. The issuer sends the payment card to the cardholder separately from the PIN mailer.
3. The cardholder uses the payment card at a merchant location. The cardholder enters the PIN into the terminal PIN pad, and the PIN is immediately encrypted using the terminal PIN encryption key (TPK). The transactional data and the encrypted PIN are transmitted to the merchant system.

    Note that the TPK is changed periodically using the key encryption key (KEK).
4. The merchant performs a PIN translation within a hardware security module (HSM), decrypting the PIN using the TPK and re-encrypting the PIN using the merchant PIN encryption key (MPK). An authorization request message with the encrypted PIN is sent to the acquirer.

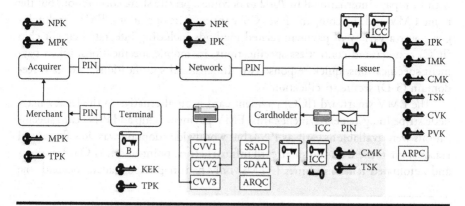

Figure 9.2   EMV payment card.

5. The acquirer performs another PIN translation within an HSM, decrypting the PIN using the MPK and re-encrypting the PIN using the network PIN encryption key (NPK). The authorization request is forwarded to the payment network.
6. The network performs another PIN translation within an HSM, decrypting the PIN using the NPK and re-encrypting the PIN using the issuer PIN encryption key. The network routes the request to the issuer for authorization.
7. The issuer verifies the PIN using the PVK, checks the cardholder profile, and returns an authorization response message to the network, acquirer, and merchant.

Regardless of whether the payment is magstripe based or EMV based the online PIN verification is the same. Online EMV authorizations operate per the following steps.

1. The issuer uses an issuer master key (IMK) to derive a unique card master key (CMK) with the card's primary account number (PAN), and the CMK is injected into the card.
2. The issuer sends the EMV card to the cardholder.
3. The cardholder uses the card at a merchant location.
4. The EMV card uses the CMK to derive a unique transaction session key (TSK) with the application transaction counter and uses the TSK to generate an Authorization Request Cryptogram (ARQC) with the transaction data. The transactional data and the ARQC is transmitted to the merchant system. See Figure 9.3.
5. An authorization request message with the ARQC is sent to the acquirer.
6. The authorization request with the ARQC is forwarded to the payment network.

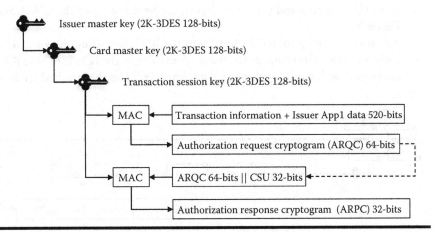

Figure 9.3 Authorization request and response.

7. The network routes the authorization request with the ARQC to the issuer for authorization.
8. The issuer uses the IMK to re-derive the CMK and then uses the CMK to derive the unique TSK which is then used to verify the ARQC. The TSK is then reused with the ARQC to generate an Authorization Response Cryptogram (ARPC). The issuer returns an authorization response message with the ARPC to the network, acquirer, and merchant. See Figure 9.3.

In addition to online authorization, EMV supports offline authorizations. The EMV terminal performs authorization: the merchant, acquirer, network, and issuer do not receive an online authorization message. EMV does not use X.509 certificates but employs a proprietary PKI credential. Offline EMV authorizations operate per the following steps.

1. The issuer generates an Rivest–Shamir–Adleman (RSA) key pair, obtains a credential signed by the brand (B) CA, and installs the issuer (I) credential into an ICC card.
2. The issuer signs the static application data (SAD) object using the issuer private key installs the signed static application data (SSAD) into the ICC card. See Figure 9.4.
3. The issuer generates another RSA key pair, creates an ICC credential signed by its issuer (I) private key, and installs the ICC credential and ICC private key into the ICC card.
4. The issuer sends the EMV card to the cardholder.
5. The cardholder uses the card at a merchant location.
6. Optionally, the terminal authenticates the ICC card using static data authentication (SDA). The issuer (I) credential and SSAD are sent from the ICC card to the terminal. The terminal uses the brand (B) credential to verify the issuer (I) credential and then the issuer (I) credential to verify the SSAD. See Figure 9.4.
7. Alternatively, the terminal authenticates the ICC card using dynamic data authentication. The terminal sends a random value to the ICC card. The ICC card signs the dynamic application data (which includes the terminal random

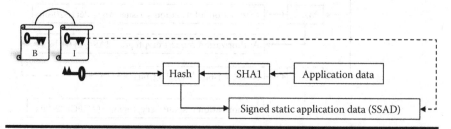

Figure 9.4   Static data authentication.

value) using the ICC private key and sends the signed dynamic application data (SDAD) to the terminal for verification. The terminal uses the brand (B) credential to verify the issuer (I) credential, uses the issuer (I) credential to verify the ICC credential, and uses the ICC credential to verify the SDAD. See Figure 9.5.

8. For offline PIN verification, the ICC card verifies the PIN. The ICC credential is sent to the terminal. The terminal uses the brand (B) credential to verify the issuer (I) credential and then uses the issuer (I) credential to verify the ICC credential. The cardholder enters the PIN into the terminal PIN pad, and the PIN is immediately encrypted by the terminal using the ICC credential. The encrypted PIN is sent from the terminal to the ICC card where it is decrypted and verified.

Another legacy card validation mechanism is the card integrity code; each brand has its own term but all use the same proprietary algorithms. Visa[*] and Discover[†] use the term card verification value (CVV), MasterCard[‡] calls it a card validation code, American Express[§] refers to card security code (CSC), and Japan Credit Bureau (JCB)[¶] uses the term card authentication value. The term CVV is used in Figure 9.2. The CVV is generated using a CVV validation key with three data inputs: the card PAN, expiration date, and card service code; the latter being a value designated by the brands. There are three different CVV on each card.

- CVV1 is encoded onto the magnetic stripe. This variation uses the PAN, expiration date, and the card service code.
- CVV2 is printed in the signature panel. This version uses the PAN, expiration date, and a special card service code.

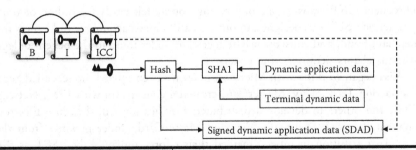

Figure 9.5   Dynamic data authentication.

[*] https://usa.visa.com
[†] https://www.discover.com
[‡] https://www.mastercard.com
[§] https://www.americanexpress.com
[¶] https://www.jcbusa.com

■ CVV3 is installed in the ICC. This algorithm uses the PAN, expiration date, and another CSC for EMV.

The issuer can verify CVV1 for legacy magstripe transaction, and CVV3 for EMV transactions, but transaction is either magstripe or EMV but never both. CVV2 is used by mail order or telephone order merchants, or for Internet (e.g., browser, mobile) merchants when the cardholder enters the PAN and expiration date. When neither the magstripe nor the ICC data is captured by a POS or EMV terminal it is considered a card-not-present (CNP) transaction; the CVV2 is entered by the cardholder for additional security.

While the four examples described do not address all of the payment authorization options and cryptography supported by EMV cards, the discussion provides a reasonable overview. Online PIN verification with the issuer provides stronger authentication. Online EMV authorization with the issuer reduces fraud but requires terminal connectivity. Offline EMV authorization with offline PIN verification is weaker than online but does not require terminal connectivity. CNP transactions are at higher risk and tend to incur the most fraud.

9.3 Secure Electronic Transactions (SET)

Secure Electronic Transactions (SET) was a joint venture between MasterCard and Visa consisting of technical specifications and an operational organization (SETCo). The World Wide Web opened the Internet in the early 1990s to anyone with a browser (e.g., Netscape, Mosaic) and a network connection. The primary SET business driver was fraudulent merchants; fraudsters posing as legitimate merchants to gather card information (e.g., PAN, expiration date, CCV2, PIN) for subsequent CNP transactions or creating counterfeit cards for online or offline transactions. SET was designed to protect cardholders, acquirers, and issuers from merchant fraud, and consequently reduce cardholder fraud to the benefit of legitimate merchants, acquirers, and issuers.

Visa began working with Microsoft to create a centralized model called Secure Transaction Technology. MasterCard created a consortium with IBM, Netscape, GTE, and others to develop a distributed specification called Secure Electronic Payment Protocol. Eventually Visa and MasterCard, under pressure from their financial institution members, merged their efforts and published SET as three books: (1) Business Description [99], (2) Programmer's Guide [100], and (3) Formal Protocol Definition [101].

All three books were developed with advice and assistance provided by GTE, IBM, Microsoft, Netscape, RSA, Science Applications International Corporation (SAIC), Terisa, and VeriSign. Many individuals from other companies who participated in the manufacturing or deployment of SET included (in alphabetical order) American Express, CertCo, Digital Signature Trust, Fisher International, KMPG

LLP, and Nortel. Visa and MasterCard established SETCo, a legal entity to specifically manage SET participants and affiliations, in the hopes that other brands
(e.g., American Express) would join; however, no other brands officially became
members. After operating worldwide for six years, SET was decommissioned in
2002. See Figure 9.6.

The SET scheme has three processing environments: the cardholder, the merchant, and the gateway. Transactions originate with the cardholder, sent to the merchant, forwarded to the gateway, and transmitted to a legacy payments network.
SET was based on a global PKI, the SETCo root CA (SET) was operated offline
at an undisclosed location; its technical details was a closely guarded secret. See
Figure 9.7.

Each participating brand (e.g., Visa, MasterCard) operated a brand CA (BCA)
whose certificate was signed by the SETCo root CA. Each BCA had regional CA
around the world, including Japan, the United States, Denmark, and France,
whose certificates were signed by the associated BCA. Each regional CA issued
certificates to a cardholder CA (CCA), a merchant CA (MCA), and a gateway CA
(GCA). The CCA issued certificates to cardholders, the MCA issued certificates to
merchants, and the GCA issued certificates to gateways. Consequently, cardholders, merchants, and gateways had separate certificate chains for each brand (Visa,
MasterCard). The SET cryptography operates as follows.

1. The cardholder signs the purchase data (e.g., red sweater size XL, priced at
   $30, customer name, customer address, shipping address) using its private
   key and encrypts the signed data using the merchant's certificate.

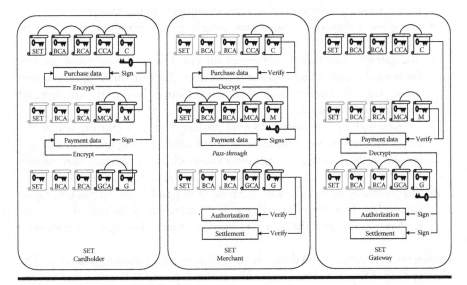

Figure 9.6 SET cryptography.

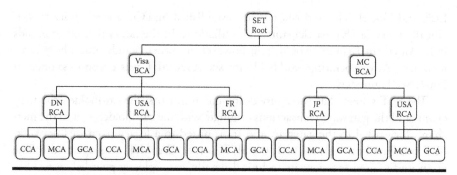

Figure 9.7   SET certification authority.

2. The cardholder signs the payment data (e.g., PAN, expiration date, CVV2) using its private key and encrypts the signed data using the gateway's certificate.
3. The cardholder sends both signed and encrypted objects to the merchant.
4. The merchant decrypts the purchase data using its private key and verifies the signature using the cardholder's certificate.
5. The merchant re-signs the encrypted signed payment data using its private key and forwards the doubly signed encrypted object to the gateway; the merchant cannot decrypt the encrypted signed payment data.
6. The gateway verifies the merchant signature using the merchant's certificate, decrypts the payment object using its private key, and verifies the cardholder signature using the cardholder's certificate.
7. The gateway uses the payment data to send an authorization request to a legacy payment network and receives an authorization response.
8. The gateway signs the authorization using its private key and returns it to the merchant.
9. The gateway sends daily settlement information to the payment gateway for normal clearing and settlement processes. The settlement process moves money from the issuer (who in turn bills the cardholder) to the acquirer and the merchant's account.

    Alternatively, for merchants who process their own clearing and settlement, the gateway signs the settlement information using its private key and sends it to the merchant. The gateway knows when to provide settlement info to the merchant based on a settlement flag in the merchant's certificate.
10. The merchant verifies the authorization (and possibly the settlement) signatures using the gateway's certificate. If the merchant is authorized to receive settlement info, then the merchant handles its own clearing and settlement.

During the development and deployment of SET, another technology developed by Netscape called Secure Socket Lay (SSL) was also deployed in browsers and servers. As discussed in Chapter 5, SSL was the predecessor to TLS. SSL and eventually

TLS overcame SET due to three significant issues: cardholder authentication, merchant authentication, and merchant settlement.

- Cardholder authentication was lacking, as SET rarely issued cardholder certificates. The cardholder relationship is with the issuer; for MasterCard and Visa, the issuers are financial institutions. However, banks were not prepared to provide federated identity of its customers to any relying party (e.g., merchants, gateways, acquires, networks).
- Merchant authentication was available using other methods. Acquirers and gateways have contractual agreements with their merchants; vetting merchants is business as usual and part of the business due diligence. Fraudulent merchants seemed to be less of an issue than originally envisioned. However, hacking and data breaches have apparently overtaken the fraudulent merchant threat with hacked merchant.
- Merchant settlement was enabled, as SET regularly allowed gateways to send settlement information back to large merchants. Large merchants were better suited to deploy SET but typically process their own settlement. Thus, large merchants gained access to the payment data from the settlement information.

When cardholder signatures are eliminated, the connection to the merchant is just encryption, basically the same as SSL or TLS. When merchant signatures are negated by other business due diligence, the connection to the gateways is just encryption, again the same as SSL or TLS. And since settlement information returned by the gateway provides payment data to the merchant, this is basically the same result as the cardholder encrypting card data to the merchant using SSL or TLS. Hence, SET, which was complicated and expensive to use, was basically reduced to the security equivalent of SSL or TLS which is simpler and cheaper to operate.

9.4 ATM Remote Key Load (RKL)

ATMs in the 1980s only had symmetric keys; it was not until the 1990s when asymmetric keys became available. ATM had two keys [102] denoted A-key and B-key*. The B-key was known as the communication key, used for PIN encryption. The A-key was called the terminal master key, basically a KEK used to exchange B-keys. However, ATMs have since been upgraded using Encryption PIN Pad (EPP) as per the directives from the Payment Card Industry Security Standards Council[†] (PCI SSC).

---

* https://www.visadps.com/download/ATM-Terminal-Driving-Service-Overview.pdf
† https://www.pcisecuritystandards.org/

PCI SSC was founded in 2006 by American Express, Discover Financial Services, JCB International, MasterCard, and Visa as a collaboration for common security programs. One of the many security standards and programs is the EPP Security Requirements [103]. The requirements address device characteristics consisting of physical security and logical security, and device management during manufacturing and between manufacturing and initial key loading. Figure 9.8 shows an ATM remote key loading (RKL) process and the subsequent PIN processing for three types of transactions: on-us, foreign card, and foreign ATM.

The RKL discussed in Figure 9.8 consists of the host loading initial cryptographic keys into empty EPP provided by the manufacturer's key management service (KMS). The KMS provides an EPP key file (EKF) to the new owners (host), so keys can be initialized into multiple EPPs that are installed in various ATMs. RKL consists of the following steps:

1. The host and KMS exchange public keys using a variety of possible methods including portable media or electronic transmission. Alternatively, the two entities exchange X.509 public key certificates.
2. The host and KMS exchange and verify the hash of each public key to verify the integrity of the public keys. Certificates are not used. Alternatively, each entity validates the certificate of the other entity.
3. The KMS generates different asymmetric keys unique per EPP and creates an EKF containing the EPP serial numbers and asymmetric keys.
4. The KMS signs the EKF using its private key and encrypts the signed EKF using the host public key. The encrypted signed EKF is transmitted to the host.
5. The host decrypts the EKF using its private key and verifies the signature using the KMS public key.

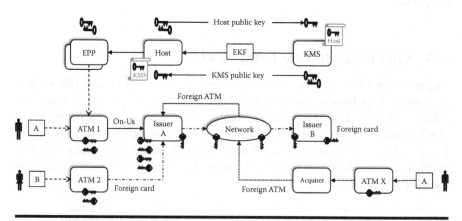

Figure 9.8   ATM remote key load.

6. The host loads the unique keys per EPP using the EKF into the designated EPP and installs the active devices into the various ATMs to enable PIN encryption.

Once each ATM has an active EPP it can remotely load the A-key using the EPP asymmetric keys, and then remotely load the B-key using the A-key. The ATM can then accept and encrypt a cardholder PIN. For an issuer that operates an ATM, there are three different types of transactions: on-us transactions, foreign card transactions, and foreign ATM transactions. Figure 9.8 shows an on-us transaction when the cardholder uses a card (A) at the issuer's (A) ATM.

1. The host generates a symmetric A-key, encrypts it using the EPP public key, and remotely loads the encrypted A-key into the EPP. The EPP decrypts and installs the A-key terminal master key.
2. The host generates a symmetric B-key, encrypts it using the A-key, and remotely loads the encrypted B-key into the EPP. The EPP decrypts and installs the B-key communication key.
3. The cardholder inserts the card (A) into ATM 1 and enters the PIN.
4. The ATM encrypts the PIN using its PIN encryption key (PEK) and sends it onto the host system (Issuer A) along with the PAN and other transaction data.
5. The host system recognizes the PAN, decrypts the PIN for verification, and authorizes the cardholder to complete the ATM transaction.

Figure 9.8 also depicts a foreign card transaction when the cardholder uses a card (B) at the issuer's (A) ATM. The transaction needs to be authorized by the appropriate issuer (B).

1. The cardholder inserts the card (B) into ATM 2 and enters the PIN.
2. The ATM encrypts the PIN using its PEK and sends it onto the host system (Issuer A) along with the PAN and other transaction data.
3. The host system does not recognize the PAN, so the PIN is translated from the ATM key to the network key, and sends an authorization request to the network.
4. The network translates the PIN from the key shared with issuer A to the key shared with issuer B, and routes the request to issuer B.
5. Issuer B decrypts the PIN for verification, authorizes the cardholder transaction, and returns an authorization response.
6. The network returns the response to issuer A for completing the ATM transaction.

Figure 9.8 further shows a foreign ATM transaction when the cardholder uses a card (A) at the issuer's (B) ATM. The transaction needs to be authorized by the appropriate issuer (A).

1. The cardholder inserts the card (A) into ATM X and enters the PIN.
2. The ATM encrypts the PIN using its PEK and sends it onto the host system (issuer B) along with the PAN and other transaction data.
3. The host system (B) does not recognize the PAN, so the PIN is translated from the ATM key to the network key, and sends an authorization request to the network.
4. The network translates the PIN from the key shared with issuer B to the key shared with issuer A, and routes the request to issuer A.
5. Issuer A decrypts the PIN for verification, authorizes the cardholder transaction, and returns an authorization response.
6. The network returns the response to issuer B for completing the ATM transaction.

The transactions discussed in this section are for online PIN verification and the process for loading keys into an EPP. Once the asymmetric keys are loaded into an EPP, the A-key and B-key can be remotely loaded into the EPP. New B-keys can be exchanged as often as required using the A-key. Similarly, new A-keys can be exchanged as often as needed using the EPP asymmetric keys. The asymmetric keys remain static for the lifetime of the EPP.

9.5 Database Encryption (DBE)

DBE has emerged as a data protection mechanism to prevent unauthorized disclosure of information. Stolen media only contains encrypted data which cannot be decrypted without the data encryption key (DEK). Unauthenticated access to storage media which bypasses access controls only enables downloading encrypted data, which again cannot be decrypted without the key. Consequently, DBE is one layer for a defense in depth approach to protect networks, servers, DBs, and information. However, the DEK might be managed in a variety of methods using software and hardware cryptography. Figure 9.9 depicts a DB server using encryption, the DB keys managed by a KMS, and the KMS server using an HSM.

Further, as shown in Figure 9.9, encryption can be applied at several levels: disk encryption, DBE, table encryption, or column encryption.

- **Disk encryption** uses a DEK to encipher the whole disk irrespective of the file system or any DB. The disk is enciphered during system shutdown and deciphered during system start-up. This protects the disk if lost or stolen but does not offer protection when the system is running.
- **Database encryption** uses a DEK to encipher the whole DB regardless of any tables or columns. The DB is initially enciphered, sections are deciphered in memory as needed, and re-enciphered to disk according to need. This

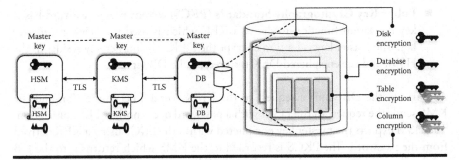

Figure 9.9   Database encryption.

protects the DB from unauthenticated access. Authenticated access automatically deciphers the DB sections into memory.

■ **Table encryption** uses a DEK to encipher a specific table within a DB regardless of its columns. The table is initially enciphered, sections are deciphered in memory as needed, and re-enciphered to disk according to need. This protects the table from unauthenticated access. Authenticated access automatically deciphers the table sections into memory.

■ **Column encryption** uses a DEK to encipher a specific column within a DB table. The column is initially enciphered, sections are deciphered in memory as needed, and re-enciphered to disk according to need. This protects the column from unauthenticated access. Authenticated access automatically deciphers the column sections into memory.

Regardless of the DBE method the DEK typically resides in the memory of server. The DEK is often stored encrypted on the server using a master key such that the DEK can be decrypted for use in memory. However, the master key is not stored on the DB server; rather the master key is provided to the DB server from either a KMS or possibly an HSM. The method used to transport the master key to the DB server varies widely among DB providers and third-party DBE providers. Many of these key transport methods were discussed in Chapter 3.

■ **Faux key** misuses a data object as a cryptographic key. The DEK is encrypted using a faux key. The faux key is encrypted using a master key that resides only in the HSM. The enciphered faux key and the enciphered DEK are stored on the DB server.

At start-up, the DB sends the enciphered faux key to the KMS over a TLS connection and the KMS sends it to the HSM over another TLS connection. The HSM decrypts the faux key using the master key, unawares the data object is being misused as a faux key. The HSM returns the cleartext faux key to the KMS and the KMS returns it to the DB server. The DB server decrypts the DEK using the faux key in memory.

- **Public Key Cryptography Standards (PKCS) tokens** uses a password-based key derivation function to derive a KEK which is used to encipher a master key. The master key is used to encrypt the DEK. The master key resides in the HSM, and the enciphered DEK is stored on the DB server.

At start-up, the DB sends a request to the KMS over a TLS connection and the KMS sends the request to the HSM with a password over another TLS connection. The HSM exports the master key enciphered within the PKCS using a KEK derived from the password. The PKCS is returned to the KMS which returns it to the DB server. The password might be stored on the DB server or provided by the KMS to the DB server. The DB server uses the password to open the PKCS and decrypt the DEK using the master key in memory.

- Database Encryption Key Management uses HMAC within an HSM to generate a seed that is subsequently an input to a key derivation function (KDF) on the DB server to generate a DEK. The HSM provides an HMAC key (HK) encrypted using a master key. The master key resides in the HSM and the enciphered HK is stored on the DB server.

At start-up, the DB sends a request to the KMS over a TLS connection with the enciphered HK and a unique database identifier (ID). The KM sends the items to the HSM. The HSM decrypts the HK using the master key and generates a seed using HMAC with the HK and ID as inputs. The seed is returned to the KMS and the DB server. The DB server generates the DEK in memory using a KDF.

Annex Quick References

ASCII and EBCDIC Quick Reference

The following table* provides both American Standard Code for Information Interchange (ASCII) and Extended Binary Coded Decimal Interchange Code (EBCDIC) symbols, descriptions, and values in binary and hexadecimal notations. ASCII is a 7-bit encoding scheme so only has an alphabet for hex values 00 through 7F. EBCDIC is an 8-bit encoding scheme and so has an alphabet for hex 00 through FF. Note that not every hex value has a corresponding ASCII or EBCDIC value.

Binary	Hex	ASCII	ASCII Description	EBCDIC	EBCDIC Description
0000 0000	00	NUL	Null	NUL	Null
0000 0001	01	SOH	Start of heading	SOH	Start of heading
0000 0010	02	STX	Start of text	STX	Start of text
0000 0011	03	ETX	End of text	ETX	End of text
0000 0100	04	EOT	End of transmission	SEL	Select
0000 0101	05	ENQ	Enquiry	HT	Horizontal tab
0000 0110	06	ACK	Acknowledge	RNL	Required new line
0000 0111	07	BEL	Bell	DEL	Delete
0000 1000	08	BS	Backspace	GE	Graphic escape

(Continued)

---

* www.ibm.com/support/knowledgecenter/en/SSGH4D_15.1.2/com.ibm.xlf151.aix.doc/language_ref/asciit.html

Binary	Hex	ASCII	ASCII Description	EBCDIC	EBCDIC Description
0000 1001	09	HT	Horizontal tab	SPS	Superscript
0000 1010	0A	LF	Line feed	RPT	Repeat
0000 1011	0B	VT	Vertical tab	VT	Vertical tab
0000 1100	0C	FF	Form feed	FF	Form feed
0000 1101	0D	CR	Carriage return	CR	Carriage return
0000 1110	0E	SO	Shift out	SO	Shift out
0000 1111	0F	SI	Shift in	SI	Shift in
0001 0000	10	DLE	Data link escape	DLE	Data link escape
0001 0001	11	DC1	Device control 1	DC1	Device control 1
0001 0010	12	DC2	Device control 2	DC2	Device control 2
0001 0011	13	DC3	Device control 3	DC3	Device control 3
0001 0100	14	DC4	Device control 4	RES/ENP	Restore/enable presentation
0001 0101	15	NAK	Negative acknowledge	NL	New line
0001 0110	16	SYN	Synchronous idle	BS	Backspace
0001 0111	17	ETB	End of transmission block	POC	Program operator communications
0001 1000	18	CAN	Cancel	CAN	Cancel
0001 1001	19	EM	End of medium	EM	End of medium
0001 1010	1A	SUB	Substitute	UBS	Unit backspace
0001 1011	1B	ESC	Escape	CU1	Customer use 1
0001 1100	1C	FS	File separator	IFS	Interchange file separator
0001 1101	1D	GS	Group separator	IGS	Interchange group separator
0001 1110	1E	RS	Record separator	IRS	Interchange record separator

(Continued)

Binary	Hex	ASCII	ASCII Description	EBCDIC	EBCDIC Description
0001 1111	1F	US	Unit separator	IUS/ITB	Interchange unit separator/ intermediate transmission block
0010 0000	20	SP	Space	DS	Digit select
0010 0001	21	!	Exclamation mark	SOS	Start of significance
0010 0010	22	"	Straight double quotation mark	FS	Field separator
0010 0011	23	#	Number sign	WUS	Word underscore
0010 0100	24	$	Dollar sign	BYP/INP	Bypass/inhibit presentation
0010 0101	25	%	Percent sign	LF	Line feed
0010 0110	26	&	Ampersand	ETB	End of transmission block
0010 0111	27	'	Apostrophe	ESC	Escape
0010 1000	28	(	Left parenthesis	SA	Set attribute
0010 1001	29	)	Right parenthesis		
0010 1010	2A	*	Asterisk	SM/SW	Set model switch
0010 1011	2B	+	Addition sign	CSP	Control sequence prefix
0010 1100	2C	,	Comma	MFA	Modify field attribute
0010 1101	2D	–	Subtraction sign	ENQ	Enquiry
0010 1110	2E	.	Period	ACK	Acknowledge
0010 1111	2F	/	Right slash	BEL	Bell
0011 0000	30	0			
0011 0001	31	1			
0011 0010	32	2		SYN	Synchronous idle
0011 0011	33	3		IR	Index return

(Continued)

Binary	Hex	ASCII	ASCII Description	EBCDIC	EBCDIC Description
0011 0100	34	4		PP	Presentation position
0011 0101	35	5		TRN	
0011 0110	36	6		NBS	Numeric backspace
0011 0111	37	7		EOT	End of transmission
0011 1000	38	8		SBS	Subscript
0011 1001	39	9		IT	Indent tab
0011 1010	3A	:	Colon	RFF	Required form feed
0011 1011	3B	;	Semicolon	CU3	Customer use 3
0011 1100	3C	<	Less than	DC4	Device control 4
0011 1101	3D	=	Equal	NAK	Negative acknowledge
0011 1110	3E	>	Greater than		
0011 1111	3F	?	Question mark	SUB	Substitute
0100 0000	40	@	At symbol	SP	Space
0100 0001	41	A			
0100 0010	42	B			
0100 0011	43	C			
0100 0100	44	D			
0100 0101	45	E			
0100 0110	46	F			
0100 0111	47	G			
0100 1000	48	H			
0100 1001	49	I			
0100 1010	4A	J		¢	Cent

(Continued)

Binary	Hex	ASCII	ASCII Description	EBCDIC	EBCDIC Description
0100 1011	4B	K		.	Period
0100 1100	4C	L		<	Less than
0100 1101	4D	M		(	Left parenthesis
0100 1110	4E	N		+	Addition sign
0100 1111	4F	O		|	Logical or
0101 0000	50	P		&	Ampersand
0101 0001	51	Q			
0101 0010	52	R			
0101 0011	53	S			
0101 0100	54	T			
0101 0101	55	U			
0101 0110	56	V			
0101 0111	57	W			
0101 1000	58	X			
0101 1001	59	Y			
0101 1010	5A	Z		!	Exclamation mark
0101 1011	5B	[	Left bracket	$	dollar sign
0101 1100	5C	\	Left slash	*	Asterisk
0101 1101	5D	]	Right bracket	)	Right parenthesis
0101 1110	5E	^	Hat, circumflex	;	Semicolon
0101 1111	5F	_	Underscore	¬	Logical not
0110 0000	60	`	Grave	−	Subtraction sign
0110 0001	61	a		/	Right slash
0110 0010	62	b			
0101 0011	63	c			
0110 0100	64	d			

(Continued)

Binary	Hex	ASCII	ASCII Description	EBCDIC	EBCDIC Description
0110 0101	65	e			
0110 0110	66	f			
0110 0111	67	g			
0110 1000	68	h			
0110 1001	69	i			
0110 1010	6A	j		|	Split vertical bar
0110 1011	6B	k		,	Comma
0110 1100	6C	l		%	Percent sign
0110 1101	6D	m		_	Underscore
0110 1110	6E	n		>	Greater than
0110 1111	6F	o		?	Question mark
0111 0000	70	p			
0111 0001	71	q			
0111 0010	72	r			
0111 0011	73	s			
0111 0100	74	t			
0111 0101	75	u			
0111 0110	76	v			
0111 0111	77	w			
0111 1000	78	x			
0111 1001	79	y		`	Grave
0111 1010	7A	z		:	Colon
0111 1011	7B	{	Left brace	#	Number sign
0111 1100	7C	|	Logical or	@	At symbol
0111 1101	7D	}	Right brace	'	Apostrophe
0111 1110	7E	~	Similar, tilde	=	Equal

(Continued)

Binary	Hex	ASCII	ASCII Description	EBCDIC	EBCDIC Description
0111 1111	7F	DEL	Delete	"	Straight double quotation mark
1000 0000	80				
1000 0001	81			a	
1000 0010	82			b	
1000 0011	83			c	
1000 0100	84			d	
1000 0101	85			e	
1000 0110	86			f	
1000 0111	87			g	
1000 1000	88			h	
1000 1001	89			i	
1000 1010	8A				
1000 1011	8B				
1000 1100	8C				
1000 1101	8D				
1000 1110	8E				
1000 1111	8F				
1001 0000	90				
1001 0001	91			j	
1001 0010	92			k	
1001 0011	93			l	
1001 0100	94			m	
1001 0101	95			n	
1001 0110	96			o	
1001 0111	97			p	

(Continued)

Binary	Hex	ASCII	ASCII Description	EBCDIC	EBCDIC Description
1001 1000	98			q	
1001 1001	99			r	
1001 1010	9A				
1001 1011	9B				
1001 1100	9C				
1001 1101	9D				
1001 1110	9E				
1001 1111	9F				
1010 0000	A0				
1010 0001	A1			~	Similar, tilde
1010 0010	A2			s	
1010 0011	A3			T	
1010 0100	A4			U	
1010 0101	A5			V	
1010 0110	A6			w	
1010 0111	A7			x	
1010 1000	A8			y	
1010 1001	A9			z	
1010 1010	AA				
1010 1011	AB				
1010 1100	AC				
1010 1101	AD				
1010 1110	AE				
1010 1111	AF				
1011 0000	B0				
1011 0001	B1				

(Continued)

Binary	Hex	ASCII	ASCII Description	EBCDIC	EBCDIC Description
1011 0010	B2				
1011 0011	B3				
1011 0100	B4				
1011 0101	B5				
1011 0110	B6				
1011 0111	B7				
1011 1000	B8				
1011 1001	B9				
1011 1010	BA				
1011 1011	BB				
1011 1100	BC				
1011 1101	BD				
1011 1110	BE				
1011 1111	BF				
1100 0000	C0			{	Left brace
1100 0001	C1			A	
1100 0010	C2			B	
1100 0011	C3			C	
1100 0100	C4			D	
1100 0101	C5			E	
1100 0110	C6			F	
1100 0111	C7			G	
1100 1000	C8			H	
1100 1001	C9			I	
1100 1010	CA				
1100 1011	CB				

(Continued)

Binary	Hex	ASCII	ASCII Description	EBCDIC	EBCDIC Description
1100 1100	CC				
1100 1101	CD				
1100 1110	CE				
1100 1111	CF				
1101 0000	D0			}	Right brace
1101 0001	D1			J	
1101 0010	D2			K	
1101 0011	D3			L	
1101 0100	D4			M	
1101 0101	D5			N	
1101 0110	D6			O	
1101 0111	D7			P	
1101 1000	D8			Q	
1101 1001	D9			R	
1101 1010	DA				
1101 1011	DB				
1101 1100	DC				
1101 1101	DD				
1101 1110	DE				
1101 1111	DF				
1110 0000	E0			\	Left slash
1110 0001	E1				
1110 0010	E2			S	
1110 0011	E3			T	
1110 0100	E4			U	
1110 0101	E5			V	

(Continued)

Binary	Hex	ASCII	ASCII Description	EBCDIC	EBCDIC Description
1110 0110	E6			W	
1110 0111	E7			X	
1110 1000	E8			Y	
1110 1001	E9			Z	
1110 1010	EA				
1110 1011	EB				
1110 1100	EC				
1110 1101	ED				
1110 1110	EE				
1110 1111	EF				
1111 0000	F0			0	
1111 0001	F1			1	
1111 0010	F2			2	
1111 0011	F3			3	
1111 0100	F4			4	
1111 0101	F5			5	
1111 0110	F6			6	
1111 0111	F7			7	
1111 1000	F8			8	
1111 1001	F9			9	
1111 1010	FA					Vertical line
1111 1011	FB				
1111 1100	FC				
1111 1101	FD				
1111 1110	FE				
1111 1111	FF			EO	Eight ones

Base64 Quick Reference

The following table[†] provides Base64 encoding alphanumeric uppercase and lowercase displayable characters, and values in decimal, 6-bit binary, and hexadecimal notations. In addition to the 6-bit binary mapping to the Base64 character there are encoding rules. The encoding results need to be a multiple of three bytes such that the last 24-bits appear as one of the following:

- Three ASCII characters encoded as 8-bit values (despite the fact that ASCII only uses the rightmost 7-bits)
- Two ASCII characters encoded as 8-bit values with 8 binary zeros
- One ASCII character encoded as an 8-bit value with 16 binary zeros

For two ASCII characters the eight binary zeros are encoded as one displayable "=" equal character. For one ASCII character the 16 binary zeroes are encoded as two displayable "= =" equal characters. Note that the equal character is not included in the table.

Base64 encoders and decoders can be found online[‡] to translate characters.

Binary	Hex	Decimal	Character
00 0000	00	0	A
00 0001	01	1	B
00 0010	02	2	C
00 0011	03	3	D
00 0100	04	4	E
00 0101	05	5	F
00 0110	06	6	G
00 0111	07	7	H
00 1000	08	8	I
00 1001	09	9	J
00 1010	0A	10	K

(Continued)

[†] RFC 4648 The Base16, Base32, and Base64 Data Encodings, October 2006.
[‡] www.base64encode.org/

Binary	Hex	Decimal	Character
00 1011	0B	11	L
00 1100	0C	12	M
00 1101	0D	13	N
00 1110	0E	14	O
00 1111	0F	15	P
01 0000	10	16	Q
01 0001	11	17	R
01 0010	12	18	S
01 0011	13	19	T
01 0100	14	20	U
01 0101	15	21	V
01 0110	16	22	W
01 0111	17	23	X
01 1000	18	24	Y
01 1001	19	25	Z
01 1010	1A	26	a
01 1011	1B	27	b
01 1100	1C	28	c
01 1101	1D	29	d
01 1110	1E	30	e
01 1111	1F	31	f
10 0000	20	32	g
10 0001	21	33	h
10 0010	22	34	i
10 0011	23	35	j
10 0100	24	36	k

(*Continued*)

Binary	Hex	Decimal	Character
10 0101	25	37	l
10 0110	26	38	m
10 0111	27	39	n
10 1000	28	40	o
10 1001	29	41	p
10 1010	2A	42	q
10 1011	2B	43	r
10 1100	2C	44	s
10 1101	2D	45	t
10 1110	2E	46	u
10 1111	2F	47	v
11 0000	30	48	w
11 0001	31	49	x
11 0010	32	50	y
11 0011	33	51	z
11 0100	34	52	0
11 0101	35	53	1
11 0110	36	54	2
11 0111	37	55	3
11 1000	38	56	4
11 1001	39	57	5
11 1010	3A	58	6
11 1011	3B	59	7
11 1100	3C	60	8
11 1101	3D	61	9
11 1110	3E	62	+
11 1111	3F	63	/

For the first example, the ASCII string "Examples" is Base64 encoded as "RXhhbXBsZXMu" shown as follows:

E	x	a	m	p	l	e	s	.
45	78	61	6D	70	6C	65	73	2E
0100 0101	0111 1000	0110 0001	0110 1101	0111 0000	0110 1100	0110 0101	0111 0011	0010 1110

The ASCII 8-bit encoded string is shown above, and the Base64 6-bit encoded string is shown below. The ASCII characters are shown in the first row, the hex notation in the second row, and the binary notation in the third row. For Base64 encoding, the ASCII 8-bit strings are regrouped into 6-bit strings, and its decimal value is used to look up the Base64 character.

01 0001	01 0111	10 0001	10 0001	01 1011	01 0111	00 0001	10 1100	01 1001	01 0111	00 1100	10 1110
17	23	33	33	27	23	1	44	25	23	12	46
R	X	H	h	b	X	B	s	Z	X	M	u

For the second example, the ASCII string "Examples" is Base64 encoded as "RXhhbXBsZXM=" shown as follows.

E	x	a	m	p	l	e	S	
45	78	61	6D	70	6C	65	73	
0100 0101	0111 1000	0110 0001	0110 1101	0111 0000	0110 1100	0110 0101	0111 0011	0000 0000

The ASCII 8-bit encoded string is shown above, and the Base64 6-bit encoded string is shown below. The ASCII characters are shown in the first row, the hex notation in the second row, and the binary notation in the third row. For Base64 encoding, the ASCII 8-bit strings are regrouped into 6-bit strings, and its decimal value is used to lookup the Base64 character, with the zero padding bits shown as one "=" equal character.

010 001	010 111	100 001	100 001	011 011	010 111	000 001	101 100	011 001	010 111	001 100	000 000
17	23	33	33	27	23	1	44	25	23	12	
R	X	h	H	b	X	B	s	Z	X	M	=

For the third example, the ASCII string "Example" is Base64 encoded as "RXhhbXBsZQ==" shown as follows.

E	X	a	m	p	l	e		
45	78	61	6D	70	6C	65		
0100 0101	0111 1000	0110 0001	0110 1101	0111 0000	0110 1100	0110 0101	0000 0000	0000 0000

The ASCII 8-bit encoded string is shown above, and the Base64 6-bit encoded string is shown below. The ASCII characters are shown in the first row, the hex notation in the second row, and the binary notation in the third row. For Base64 encoding, the ASCII 8-bit strings are regrouped into 6-bit strings, and its decimal value is used to look up the Base64 character, with the zero padding bits shown as two "= =" equal characters.

01 0001	01 0111	10 0001	10 0001	01 1011	01 0111	00 0001	10 1100	01 1001	01 0000	00 0000	00 0000
17	23	33	33	27	23	1	44	25	16		
R	X	h	h	B	X	B	s	Z	Q	=	=

XOR Quick Reference

This annex provides an overview of exclusive-or (XOR) values.

Table 1 provides XOR for hex values 0 (binary 0000) through hex 7 (binary 0111).

Table 2 provides XOR for hex values 8 (binary 1000) through F (binary 1111).

Note that XOR is still used today for key components and other cryptographic methods so the reader now has reference material. For example, to look up $7 \oplus A$ find hex 7 (binary 0111) in the first column and hex A (binary 1010) in the first row to look up the intersection (binary 1101) which is hex D so $7 \oplus A = D$ or in binary $0111 \oplus 1010 = 1101$. Another way to figure the XOR is at the bit level as follows.

	Hex	Binary			
	7	0	1	1	1
	A	1	0	1	0
$\oplus$	D	1	1	0	1

Table 1 Hex 0-F XOR 0-7

Hex	⊕	0 / 0000	1 / 0001	2 / 0010	3 / 0011	4 / 0100	5 / 0101	6 / 0110	7 / 0111
0	0000	0000	0001	0010	0011	0100	0101	0110	0111
1	0001	–	0000	0011	0010	0101	0100	0111	0110
2	0010	–	–	0000	0001	0110	0111	0100	0101
3	0011	–	–	–	0000	0111	0110	0101	0100
4	0100	–	–	–	–	0000	0001	0010	0011
5	0101	–	–	–	–	–	0000	0011	0010
6	0110	–	–	–	–	–	–	0000	0001
7	0111	–	–	–	–	–	–	–	0000
8	1000	–	–	–	–	–	–	–	–
9	1001	–	–	–	–	–	–	–	–
A	1010	–	–	–	–	–	–	–	–
B	1011	–	–	–	–	–	–	–	–
C	1100	–	–	–	–	–	–	–	–
D	1101	–	–	–	–	–	–	–	–
E	1110	–	–	–	–	–	–	–	–
F	1111	–	–	–	–	–	–	–	–

Table 2 Hex 0-F XOR 8-F

Hex	⊕	8 / 1000	9 / 1001	A / 1010	B / 1011	C / 1100	D / 1101	E / 1110	F / 1111
0	0000	1000	1001	1010	1011	1100	1101	1110	1111
1	0001	1001	1000	1011	1010	1101	1100	1111	1110
2	0010	1010	1011	1000	1001	1110	1111	1100	1101
3	0011	1011	1010	1001	1000	1100	1110	1101	1100
4	0100	1100	1101	1110	1111	1000	1001	1010	1010

(Continued)

Table 2 (*Continued*)   Hex 0-F XOR 8-F

Hex	8	9	A	B	C	D	E	F
5	0101	1101	1101	1111	1110	1011	1000	1011	1010
6	0110	1110	1111	1100	1101	1010	1011	1000	1001
7	0111	1111	1110	1101	1100	1011	1010	1001	1000
8	1000	0000	0001	0010	0011	0100	0101	0110	0111
9	1001	–	0000	1011	0010	0101	0100	0111	0110
A	1010	–	–	0000	0001	0110	0111	0100	0101
B	1011	–	–	–	0000	0111	0110	0101	0100
C	1100	–	–	–	–	0000	0001	0010	0011
D	1101	–	–	–	–	–	0000	0011	0010
E	1110	–	–	–	–	–	–	0000	0001
F	1111	–	–	–	–	–	–	–	0000

X.509 Certificate Quick Reference

This annex provides an overview of X.509 certificates and its extensions.

Certificate

The main certificate consists of three primary fields: (1) the content to be signed (TBS), (2) the digital signature algorithm for the certificate signature generated by the certification authority (CA), and (3) the actual digital signature. The TBS filed is comprised of many secondary fields including the Extensions. The Extensions field is actually a sequence of numerous extensions each of which has a unique label called an Object Identifier (OID). An OID is basically an ordered list of numbers where each position and value has specific meaning with the characteristic that every OID has unique meaning.

Certificate	
1. TBS certificate	Content to be signed by the CA
Version	Current version is "3"
Serial number	Identifier unique per CA
Signature	Algorithm ID of the CA keys
Issuer	Name of the CA

(Continued)

Validity	
• Not before	Date and time the certificate is valid
• Not after	Date and time the certificate expires
Subject	Name of the certificate owner
Subject Public Key Info	
• Algorithm	Algorithm ID of the subject's keys
• Subject public key	Public key contained in the certificate
Extensions	
• Extension ID	OID
• Critical	Error if unknown or ignore if unknown
• Extension value	Content of the extension field
2. Signature algorithm	Algorithm ID of the CA keys
3. Signature value	Digital signature of the TBS certificate

The certification authority (CA) generates a digital signature of the TBS certificate, adds the signature algorithm such as the Rivest–Shamir–Adleman (RSA) algorithm, the Digital Signature Algorithm, or the Elliptic Curve Digital Signature Algorithm, and appends the digital signature to create the certificate. The certificate signature is a cryptographic binding of the TBS certificate fields, including the various Extensions fields, and significantly the subject's name and public key.

Extensions

X.509 certificate extensions are only present in version 3 certificates. While the X.509 standard includes numerous extensions, only the more commonly implemented and useful extensions are discussed in this annex.

Authority Key Identifier

This X.509 extension contains an identification, typically an SHA-1 hash, of the CA public key corresponding to the CA private key that signed the certificate. Its purpose is to help facilitate certificate chain construction during certificate validation particularly when the CA has more than one asymmetric key pair for signing certificates. The authority key identifier (AKI) in any certificate is the subject key identifier (SKI) of the succeeding CA certificate.

Subject Key Identifier

This X.509 extension contains an identification, typically an SHA-1 hash, of the public key contained within the certificate. Its purpose is to help facilitate certificate chain construction during certificate validation. The SKI in a CA certificate is the AKI in the preceding certificate.

Key Usage

This X.509 extension defines the purpose of the public key and consequently its corresponding private key. The field has nine bits defined but typically the expressed in hexadecimal notation where each "1" bit represents a key usage type. Any combination of bits is permitted, but there are common industry practices on how to use various permutations. While the key usage field is helpful to determine the type of certificate, the extended key usage (EKU) extension is also valuable.

0	1	2	3	4	5	6	7	8	
								decipherOnly (8)	
							encipherOnly (7)		
						cRLSign (6)			
					keyCertSign (5)				
				keyAgreement (4)					
			dataEncipherment (3)						
		keyEncipherment (2)							
	nonRepudiation (1) renamed to contentCommitment								
digitalSignature (0)									

For example, a typical CA certificate has the key certificate signature (5) and the certificate revocation list (CRL) signature (6) bits sent so the key usage value is hex 06 = 0000 0110. Since the two bits are for signatures, the digital signature (0) is not needed or appropriate; however, not all CA follow the same nomenclature, so CA certificates will have differences.

As another example, a certificate for signing emails might have the digital signature (0) bit set so the key usage value would be hex 80 = 1000 0000. Conversely, a certificate for signing legal documents might have both the digital signature (0) and the non-repudiation (1) bits set so the key usage value is hex C0 = 1100 0000. However, setting the non-repudiation bit does not inherently provide non-repudiation; rather additional controls need to be implemented.

For yet another example, a certificate for key management might have the key encipherment (2) or the key agreement (4) bits set depending if the algorithm supports key transport such as the Rivest–Shamir–Adleman scheme (RSA) or key agreement such as the Diffie–Hellman (DH) or the Elliptic Curve Diffie–Hellman (ECDH) schemes. Stereotypically TLS certificate has the digital signature (0) bit for client authentication and the key encipherment (2) bit for RSA-based key transport so the key usage value is hex A0 = 1010 0000.

Extended Key Usage

This X.509 extension indicates the intended purposes for the public key, in addition to or in place of the basic key usage extension. Instead of using a bit-map, the EKU field incorporates OIDs as follows.

- Server authentication OID = 1.3.6.1.5.5.7.3.1 is for TLS with consistent key usage bit digital signature (0) and the key management bits either key encipherment (2) or key agreement (4).
- Client authentication OID = 1.3.6.1.5.5.7.3.2 is for TLS with consistent key usage bit digital signature (0) and the key management bits either key encipherment (2) or key agreement (4).
- Code signing OID = 1.3.6.1.5.5.7.3.3 is for protecting executable code using digital signatures with consistent key usage bit digital signature (0).

The EKU field has several other OID defined in the X.509 standard. The EKU field provides additional information about the certificate, the public key, and the corresponding private key. However, when the EKU field is used without the basic key usage bits, information about the keys is less and the purpose of the keys needs to be extrapolated.

Certificate Policies

This X.509 extension contains policy information for the certificate. For end-entity certificates, the extension identifies the specific policy under which the certificate was issued including the intended purposes for using the certificate. For CA certificates the extension might list the set of policies for issuing certificates; however, if the CA has no policy limits then the anyPolicy OID = 2.5.29.32.0 can be used instead. Business applications with specific policy requirements can validate this extension and reject the certificate if noncompliant. Ideally, this extension includes a uniform resource locator (URL) pointing to the Certificate Practice Statement (CPS) published by the CA.

Subject Alternative Name

This X.509 extension, the subject alternate name (SAN) contains a list of substitute identities, basically a type of "doing business as" information. Each name is equally associated with the subject public key as is the Subject. This allows a Subject to operate under more than one name, but using the same certificate and asymmetric keys.

Industry conventions now include the Subject common name (CN) in the SAN extension along with other names, and sometimes the SAN only includes the CN. Further, the SAN size has been extended to allow for hundreds of alternate names. This latter change alleviates the need for wildcard certificates where the Subject CN "*" matches any name. For example, the domain name www.example. com might be listed as *.example.com which would match sample1.example.com and sample2.example.com or any similar website. Conversely, the SAN extension would include www.example.com, sample1.example.com, and sample2.example. com but no others. The wildcard allows any equivalent match whereas the SAN extension limits matching to a specific set of names. Ironically, adding a wildcard name to a SAN extension basically defeats the purpose of using the SAN extension altogether.

Basic Constraints

This X.509 extension identifies whether the certificate subject is a CA and can further define the maximum PKI hierarchy for certificate validation. Otherwise, the certificate is an end-entity certificate whose public key cannot be used to verify a certificate signature.

Paradoxically, end-entity self-signed certificates are not CA certificates, and yet the certificate public key is used to verify the certificate signature. Despite the digital signature, a self-signed certificate cannot have data integrity or authenticity much less any non-repudiation. Any attacker can change any of the certificate information, replace the public key, and resign the certificate with a corresponding private key; the changes are undetectable. See the discussion in this annex on self-signed certificates.

CRL Distribution Points

This X.509 extension provides information to obtain CRL information. Typically, an URL points to a website where the current CRL is posted for downloading. The CRL reason flags are another set of bits.

Authority Information Access

This X.509 extension provides issuer information or access to issuer services. Issuer information might contain CA certificates to assist in determining an appropriate certificate chain. Issuer services might contain validation services such as the location of Online Certificate Status Protocol responder. The authority information access extension does not contain CRL as that information is in the CRL Distribution Points extension.

0	1	2	3	4	5	6	7	8	
									aACompromise (8)
								privilegeWithdrawn (7)	
							certificateHold (6)		
						cessationOfOperation (5)			
					superseded (4)				
				affiliationChanged (3)					
			cACompromise (2)						
		keyCompromise (1)							
	unused (0)								

Self-Signed Certificates

Self-signed certificates as subject certificates should never be used as self-sign certificates do not provide data integrity or authenticity much less non-repudiation. See Figure Annex 1 for a comparison between self-signed certificates versus CA-signed certificates. The self-signed certificate is shown on the left and the CA-signed certificate is shown on the right with a certificate chain. The CA certificates are kept within a certificate trust store, whereas the subject certificates are exchanged during an authentication or encryption protocol. The certificate trust store might be pre-populated by a browser manufacturer or installed by a system administrator onto an application server or other network device.

The CA-signed subject certificate has a signature generated by the issuer CA private key, and the corresponding issuer CA public key is used to verify the signature. The issuer CA public key is fetched from the issuer CA certificate stored in the certificate trust store. Subsequently, the issuer CA certificate has a signature

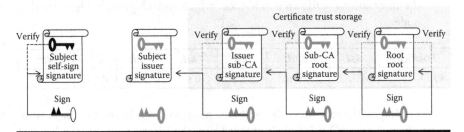

Figure Annex 1   Self-signed certificates.

generated by the sub-CA private key, and the corresponding sub-CA public key is used to verify that signature. Successively, the sub-CA certificate has a signature generated by the root CA private key, and the corresponding root CA public key is used to verify the signature. Since the root CA is the trust anchor, the root CA certificate is signed using its own private key and verified using its own public key. But, as noted, the certificate trust store has been provided by an authoritative source so the root CA "self-sign" certificate is trustworthy. Thus, when the CA-signed subject certificate is exchanged, it is validated using the CA certificate chain in the certificate trust store.

The self-signed subject certificate has a signature generated by the subject private key, and the corresponding subject public key in the certificate is used to verify the signature. There is no trustworthy certificate chain to validate the self-signed subject certificate. Thus, any attacker can copy the subject certificate, alter any information, replace the subject public key with the attacker public key, and re-sign the certificate using the attacker private key. Hence, an unsuspecting relying party receiving an unsolicited self-signed subject certificate unwittingly uses the certificate public key (subject or attacker) to verify the signature generated by the associated private key (subject or attacker).

Further, even if the relying party is provided the self-signed subject certificate over an independent communications channel but stored locally without appropriate security controls, the certificate still has no integrity. Anyone with access to the system can change and re-sign the certificate. Thus, the self-signed subject certificate is susceptible to an insider attack. Basically, a self-signed subject certificate is equivalent to a bare public key without any integrity or authenticity. Clearly, additional security controls are needed when PKI-based digital certificates are not used to protect public keys.

OID Quick Reference

This annex provides an overview of OID values. The ITU-T X.660 standard provides the following definition for an OID.

> **Object identifier**: An ordered list of primary integer values from the root of the international OID tree to a node, which unambiguously identifies that node.

Position	1st	2nd	3rd	4th	5th	6th	Nth
OID	0, 1, 2	$0 \leq n$	$0 \leq n$	$0 \leq n$	$0 \leq n$	$0 \leq n$	...

According to the scheme, each numbered position can take any integer value of 0 or greater so an OID is infinitely extensible, and as many positions can be used so an OID is infinitely expandable. This allows every OID to be globally unique.

Once defined and registered, an OID is never deleted or changed. However, more than one OID might have the same meaning. An OID is typically described as a tree structure with the ordered list beginning at the top of the tree and extending downward. Any list of numbers is called an arc. There are only three (0, 1, 2) root arcs which represent three standards organizations.

0 is ITU-T commonly written ITU-T(0)

1 is ISO commonly written ISO(1)

2 is Joint-ISO-ITU-T commonly written ISO/ITU-T(2)

The secondary ITU-T arcs are defined as follows:

ITU-T(0) Recommendation(0) also written as 0.0 arc

ITU-T(0) Administration(2) also written as 0.2 arc

ITU-T(0) Network-Operator(3) also written as 0.3 arc

ITU-T(0) Identified-Organization(4) also written as 0.4 arc

ITU-T(0) R-Recommendation(5) also written as 0.5 arc

ITU-T(0) Data(9) also written as 0.9 arc

The secondary ISO arcs are defined as follows:

ISO(1) Standard(0) also written as 1.0 arc

ISO(1) Registration-Authority(1) also written as 1.1 arc

ISO(1) Member-Body(2) also written as 1.2 arc

ISO(1) Identified-Organization(3) also written as 1.3 arc

The secondary Joint-ISO-ITU-T arcs are defined as follows:

ISO/ITU-T(2) module (1) also written as 2.1 arc

ISO/ITU-T(2) document-types(2) also written as 2.2 arc

ISO/ITU-T(2) asn-1(3) also written as 2.3 arc

ISO/ITU-T(2) international-md(5) also written as 2.5 arc

ISO/ITU-T(2) international-organization(6) also written as 2.6 arc

Examples from the RFC 5820 Internet X.509 Public Key Infrastructure (PKIX) specification include the following OID. See Annex: X.509 Certificate Quick Reference for details.

CPS Qualifier is iso (1) identified-organization(3) dod(6) internet(1) security(5) mechanisms(5) pkix(7) id-qt(2) id-qt-cps(1) or 1.3.6.1.5.5.7.2.1

Key Usage is joint-iso-ccitt(2) ds(5) id-ce(29) id-ce-keyUsage (15) or 2.5.29.15

Extended Key Usage is joint-iso-ccitt(2) ds(5) id-ce(29) id-ce-extKeyUsage(37) or 2.5.29.37

Subject Alternate Name is joint-iso-ccitt(2) ds(5) id-ce(29) id-ce-subjectAlt-Name(17) or 2.5.29.17

CRL Distribution Points is joint-iso-ccitt(2) ds(5) id-ce(29) id-ce-cRLDistributionPoints(31) or 2.5.29.31

As another example, the X9.73 Cryptographic Message Syntax (CMS) standard has its own OID per the Accredited Standards Committee X9 organization assigned from the International Standards Organization Technical Committee 68 for the financial services industry.

CMSObjectIdentifers is iso(1) identified-organization(3) tc68(133) country(16) x9(840) x9Standards(9) x9-73(73) module(0) oids(1) v2009(1) or 1.3.133.16.840.9.73.0.1.1

Each X9 standard has its own arc based on the ASC X9 arc 1.3.133.16.840.9 using its assigned number as the next value and then followed by its own OID structure.

There are several online OID registries, but none of them necessarily contain all registered OID and there is no central repository. Alternatively, any OID can be searched on the Internet with a good chance of finding an appropriate source or even a definition. OIDs are typically defined in various international and national standards, specifications, and even proprietary documents. Here are a few online OID registries.

■ Alvestrand OID Registry at www.alvestrand.no/objectid/
■ GnuPG OID Registry at www.gnupg.org/oids.html
■ Info OID Registry at www.oid-info.com/

However, many standards or specifications do not use OID, rather they use proprietary numbering systems or other identification schemes.

ASN.1 Module

This annex provides an Abstract Syntax Notation One (ASN.1) module for defining cryptographic architecture information discussed in Chapter 6. This ASN.1 module is suitable for input to programming language code generation tools. The abstract schema provided here might be used to populate a database or create a graphic interpretation of the cryptographic module information.

```
CryptographicModule ::= SEQUENCE {
    version         INTEGER,
    productInfo     ProductData,
    cryptoInfo      CryptoData,
```

```
        productCategory  ProductType,
        hostInfo         HostData,
        protocolInfo     ProtocolData
}

ProductData ::= SEQUENCE SIZE(1..MAX) OF ProductName

ProductName ::= SEQUENCE {
    manufacturer  AnyLanguage,
    make          AnyLanguage  OPTIONAL,
    model         AnyLanguage  OPTIONAL,
    number        AnyLanguage  OPTIONAL,
    nickname      AnyLanguage  OPTIONAL
}

AnyLanguage ::= UTF8String (SIZE(1..MAX))

CryptoData ::= SEQUENCE SIZE(1..MAX) OF CryptoName

CryptoName ::= SEQUENCE {
    algorithmID   AlgorithmIdentifier,
    keySizeBits   INTEGER  OPTIONAL,
    hashSizeBits  INTEGER  OPTIONAL,
    keyUse        KeyUsage,
    keyLifecycle  CryptoDates
}
KeyUsage ::= SEQUENCE SIZE(1..MAX) OF OBJECT IDENTIFIER

CryptoDates ::= SEQUENCE {
    generationDate   Time,
    useDate          Time  OPTIONAL,
    endDate          Time  OPTIONAL,
    terminationDate  Time,
    archiveDate      Time  OPTIONAL
}

Time ::= GeneralizedTime

ProductType ::= SEQUENCE {
    hardware  BOOLEAN,
    firmware  BOOLEAN,
    software  BOOLEAN,
    compiled  BOOLEAN,
    embedded  BOOLEAN,
    bundled   BOOLEAN
}

HostData ::= SEQUENCE SIZE(1..MAX) OF ProductName

ProtocolData ::= SEQUENCE SIZE(1..MAX) OF ProtocolName
```

```
ProtocolName ::= SEQUENCE {
    protocolName    AnyLanguage  OPTIONAL,
    nickname        AnyLanguage  OPTIONAL,
    protocolID      OBJECT IDENTIFIER,
    protoclVersion  INTEGER,
    parameters      OCTET STRING
}
```

Acknowledgments

Special thanks is extended to Phil Griffin for reviewing, updating, and verifying the ASN.1 syntax.

Bibliography

1. *Handbook of Applied Cryptography*, Alfred J. Menezes, Paulz C. Van Oorschot, Scott A. Vanstone, 1997, CRC Press.
2. *Applied Cryptography*, Second Edition, Bruce Schneier, 1996, John Wiley & Sons.
3. *The Code Book: The Science of Secrecy from Ancient Egypt to Quantum Cryptography*, Simon Singh, August 2000, Doubleday.
4. *Security without Obscurity: A Guide to Confidentiality, Authentication, and Integrity*, Jeff Stapleton, 2014, CRC Press Taylor & Francis Group.
5. *Security without Obscurity: A Guide to PKI Operations*, Jeff Stapleton, W. Clay Epstein, 2016, CRC Press Taylor & Francis Group.
6. *The Codebreakers: The Story of Secret Writing*, David Kahn, 1967, Macmillan Publishing Company.
7. ISO 16609, Banking – Requirements for Message Authentication Using Symmetric Techniques.
8. Federal Information Processing Standard (FIPS) Publication 198-1, The Keyed-Hash Message Authentication Code (HMAC).
9. A method for obtaining digital signatures and public-key cryptosystems, Ron L. Rivest, Adi Shamir, Martin Adleman, *Communications of the ACM*, Volume 21, Issue 2, February 1978, pp. 120–126.
10. American National Standard X9.31, Digital Signatures Using Reversible Public Key Cryptography for the Financial Services Industry (rDSA), 1998.
11. Federal Information Processing Standard (FIPS) Publication 186-4, Digital Signature Standard (DSS), July 2013.
12. American National Standard X9.62, Public Key Cryptography for the Financial Services Industry: The Elliptic Curve Digital Signature Algorithm (ECDSA), 2005.
13. ITU-T, Information Technology – Open Systems Interconnection – The Directory: Public-Key and Attribute Certificate Frameworks.
14. Digital Signature Guideline, Legal Infrastructure for Certification Authorities and Secure Electronic Commerce, Information Security Committee (ISC), Electronic Commerce and Information Technology Division, Section of Science and Technology, American Bar Association (ABA), August 1996.
15. PKI Assessment Guideline (PAG), Information Security Committee (ISC), Electronic Commerce Division, Section of Science & Technology Law, American Bar Association (ABA), June 2001.
16. CA/Browser Forum, Guidelines for the Issuance and Management of Extended Validation Certificates, Version 1.4, May 2012.

17. Trust Service Principles and Criteria for Certification Authorities, Version 2.0, March 2011, AICPA/CICA Public Key Infrastructure (PKI) Assurance Task Force.
18. CA Trust, PKI Forum Note, Jeff Stapleton, July 2001.
19. American National Standard X9.79, Public Key Infrastructure (PKI) – Part 1: Practices and Policy Framework.
20. ISO 21188, Public Key Infrastructure for Financial Services – Practices and Policy Framework.
21. Electronic Signatures in Global and National Commerce Act, Public Law 106-229 – June 30, 2000, United States Code (USC).
22. American National Standard X9.119, Retail Financial Services – Requirements for Protection of Sensitive Payment Card Data – Part 1: Using Encryption Methods.
23. American National Standard X9.119, Retail Financial Services – Requirements for Protection of Sensitive Payment Card Data – Part 2: Implementing Post-Authorization Tokenization Systems.
24. Payment Card Industry (PCI), Data Security Standard (DSS), Requirements and Security Assessment Procedures, v3.2, April 2016.
25. Payment Card Industry (PCI), Tokenization Product Security Guidelines, v1.0, April 2015.
26. Payment Card Industry (PCI), Data Security Standard (DSS), Tokenization Guidelines, v2.0, August 2011.
27. Europay-MasterCard-Visa Company (EMVCo) Payment Tokenisation Specification, Technical Framework, v1.0 March 2014.
28. American National Standard X9 TR-39-2009, TG-3 Retail Financial Services Compliance Guideline – Part 1: PIN Security and Key Management.
29. American National Standard X9.8-1-2015/ISO 9564-1-2011, Financial Services – Personal Identification Number (PIN) Management and Security – Part 1: Basic Principles and Requirements for PINs in Card-Based Systems.
30. American National Standard X9.24-1-2017. Retail Financial Services Symmetric Key Management Part 1: Using Symmetric Techniques.
31. American National Standard X9.24-2-2016. Retail Financial Service Symmetric Key Management – Part 2: Using Asymmetric Techniques for the Distribution of Symmetric Keys.
32. Public-Key Cryptography Standards (PKCS) #1: RSA Cryptography Specifications, Version 2.2, Internet Engineering Task Force (IETF), Request for Comments (RFC) 8017, November 2016.
33. Public-Key Cryptography Standards (PKCS) #5: Password-Based Cryptography Specification, Version 2.1, Internet Engineering Task Force (IETF), Request for Comments (RFC) 8018, January 2017.
34. Public-Key Cryptography Standards (PKCS) #7: Cryptographic Message Syntax, Version 1.5, Internet Engineering Task Force (IETF), Request for Comments (RFC) 2315, March 1998.
35. Public-Key Cryptography Standards (PKCS) #8: Private-Key Information Syntax Specification, Version 1.2, Internet Engineering Task Force (IETF), Request for Comments (RFC) 5208, May 2008.
36. Public-Key Cryptography Standards (PKCS) #9: Selected Object Classes and Attribute Types, Version 2.0, Internet Engineering Task Force (IETF), Request for Comments (RFC) 2985, November 2000.

37. Public-Key Cryptography Standards (PKCS) #10: Certification Request Syntax Specification, Version 1.7, Internet Engineering Task Force (IETF), Request for Comments (RFC) 2986, November 2000.

38. Public-Key Cryptography Standards (PKCS) #12: Personal Information Exchange Syntax, v1.1, Internet Engineering Task Force (IETF), Request for Comments (RFC) 7292, July 2014.

39. NIST Special Publication 800-132, Recommendation for Password-Based Key Derivation – Part 1: Storage Applications, December 2010.

40. New directions in cryptography, W. Diffie, M. Hellman, *IEEE Transactions on Information Theory*, Volume 22, No. 6, November 1976.

41. American National Standard X9.42, Public Key Cryptography for the Financial Services Industry: Agreement of Symmetric Algorithm Keys Using Diffie-Hellman, 2001.

42. American National Standard X9.44, Public-Key Cryptography for the Financial Services Industry: Key Establishment Using Integer Factorization Cryptography, 2007.

43. American National Standard X9.63, Public Key Cryptography for the Financial Services Industry: Key Agreement and Key Transport Using Elliptic Curve Cryptography, 2001.

44. OpenPGP Message Format, Internet Engineering Task Force (IETF), Request for Comments (RFC) 4880, November 2007.

45. ITU-T X.509, Information Technology – Open Systems Interconnection – The Directory: Public-Key and Attribute Certificate Frameworks.

46. ISO/IEC 9594, Information Technology – Open Systems Interconnection – The Directory – Part 8: Public-Key and Attribute Certificate Frameworks.

47. Internet X.509 Public Key Infrastructure Certificate and Certificate Revocation List (CRL) Profile, Internet Engineering Task Force (IETF), Request for Comments (RFC) 5280, May 2008.

48. ISO 3166, Codes for the Representation of Names of Countries and their Subdivisions – Part 1: Country Codes.

49. Resource Records for the DNS Security Extensions, Internet Engineering Task Force (IETF), Request for Comments (RFC) 4034, March 2005.

50. Security Issues with DNS, InfoSec Reading Room, SANS Institute, Florent Carli, 2003.

51. Domain Keys Identified Mail (DKIM) Signatures, Internet Engineering Task Force (IETF), Request for Comments (RFC) 6376, September 2011.

52. Security Assertion Markup Language (SAML) v2.0 Standard, Organization for the Advancement of Structured Information Standards (OASIS), Mach 2005.

53. Extensible Markup Language (XML) 1.0 (Fifth Edition), Word Wide Web (W3C) Consortium, W3C Recommendation 26 November 2008.

54. XML Encryption Syntax and Processing, Word Wide Web (W3C) Recommendation, December 2002.

55. The OAuth 2.0 Authorization Framework, Internet Engineering Task Force (IETF), Request for Comments (RFC) 6749, October 2012.

56. ISO 9564, Financial Services – Personal Identification Number (PIN) Management and Security – Part 1: Basic Principles and Requirements for PINs in Card-Based Systems.

57. ISO/IEC 7812, Identification Cards – Identification of issuers – Part 1: Numbering system.
58. Draft X9.132 Issuer PIN Generation, Verification, and Storage Methodologies Using AES.
59. NIST Special Publication 800-63B, Digital Identity Guidelines: Authentication and Lifecycle Management, June 2017.
60. The Secure Sockets Layer (SSL) Protocol Version 3.0, Internet Engineering Task Force (IETF), Request for Comments (RFC) 6101, August 2011.
61. The TLS Protocol Version 1.0, Internet Engineering Task Force (IETF), Request for Comments (RFC) 2246, January 1999.
62. The Transport Layer Security (TLS) Protocol Version 1.1, Internet Engineering Task Force (IETF), Request for Comments (RFC) 4346, April 2006.
63. The Transport Layer Security (TLS) Protocol Version 1.2, Internet Engineering Task Force (IETF), Request for Comments (RFC) 5246, August 2008.
64. Security Architecture for the Internet Protocol, Internet Engineering Task Force (IETF), Request for Comments (RFC) 4301, December 2005.
65. IP Authentication Header, Internet Engineering Task Force (IETF), Request for Comments (RFC) 4302, December 2005.
66. IP Encapsulating Security Payload (ESP), Internet Engineering Task Force (IETF), Request for Comments (RFC) 4303, December 2005.
67. The Secure Shell (SSH) Protocol Architecture, Internet Engineering Task Force (IETF), Request for Comments (RFC) 4251, January 2006.
68. The Secure Shell (SSH) Authentication Protocol, Internet Engineering Task Force (IETF), Request for Comments (RFC) 4252, January 2006.
69. The Secure Shell (SSH) Transport Layer Protocol, Internet Engineering Task Force (IETF), Request for Comments (RFC) 4253, January 2006.
70. The Secure Shell (SSH) Connection Protocol, Internet Engineering Task Force (IETF), Request for Comments (RFC) 4254, January 2006.
71. RSA Key Exchange for the Secure Shell (SSH) Transport Layer Protocol, Internet Engineering Task Force (IETF), Request for Comments (RFC) 4432, March 2006.
72. OpenPGP Message Format, Internet Engineering Task Force (IETF), Request for Comments (RFC) 4480, November 2007.
73. American National Standard X9.8 (Identical Adoption), ISO 9564, Personal Identification Number (PIN) Management and Security – Part 1: Basic Principles and Requirements for PIN in Card-Based Systems, 2015.
74. ISO/IEC 27002, Information Technology – Security Techniques – Code of Practice for Information Security Management.
75. NIST Special Publication 800-37, Revision 1, Guide for Applying the Risk Management Framework to Federal Information Systems, February 2010.
76. NIST Special Publication 800-40, Revision 3, Guide to Effective Remediation of Network Vulnerabilities, July 2013.
77. Qualys: Guide to Effective Remediation of Network Vulnerabilities, 2004.
78. SANS Institute InfoSec Reading Room: Steps to Vulnerability Management are Prerequisites for Proactive Protection of Business System Security, March 2013.
79. American National Standard X9.111, Penetration Testing within the Financial Services Industry, 2011.
80. Federal Information Processing Standards Publication (FIPS PUB) 140-2, Security Requirements for Cryptographic Modules, May 2001.

81. Federal Information Processing Standards Publication (FIPS PUB) 197, Advanced Encryption Standard (AES), November 2001.
82. ISO/IEC 15408, Information Technology – Security Techniques – Evaluation Criteria for IT Security – Multiple Parts, 2008.
83. ISO/IEC 19790, Information Technology – Security Techniques – Security Requirements for Cryptographic Modules.
84. American National Standard X9.97, Financial Services – Secure Cryptographic Devices (Retail) – Part 1: Concepts, Requirements and Evaluation Methods.
85. American National Standard X9.79, Public Key Infrastructure (PKI) – Part 4: Asymmetric Key Management for the Financial Services Industry.
86. American National Standard X9.82, Random Number Generation – Part 1: Overview and Basic Principles.
87. American National Standard X9.82, Random Number Generation – Part 2: Entropy Sources.
88. American National Standard X9.82, Random Number Generation – Part 3: Deterministic Random Bit Generators.
89. American National Standard X9.82, Random Number Generation – Part 4: Random Bit Generator Constructions.
90. American National Standard X9.80, Prime Number Generation, Primality Testing, and Primality Certificates.
91. PKCS #10: Certification Request Syntax Standard Version 1.0, RSA Laboratories Technical Note, November 1993.
92. NIST Special Publication 800-57, Revision 4, Recommendation for Key Management – Part 1: General.
93. X.509 Internet Public Key Infrastructure Online Certificate Status Protocol (OCSP), Internet Engineering Task Force (IETF), Request for Comments (RFC) 6960, June 2013.
94. *Cryptographic Transitions*, Jeff Stapleton, Ralph Poore, Region 5 Conference, 2006 IEEE, doi:10.1109/TPSD.2006.5507465.
95. American National Standard X9.73, Cryptographic Message Syntax (CMS) – ASN.1 and XML.
96. Secretary Donald Rumsfeld, Press Conference at NATO Headquarters, Brussels, Belgium, June 06, 2002.
97. *The Essential Writings*, William James, edited by Bruce W. Wilshire, 1971, p. xiii.
98. EMV Issuer and Application Security Guidelines, EMVCO LLC, NE31r1, Version 2.5, October 2015.
99. SET Secure Electronic Transaction Specification – Book 1: Business Description, v1.0, May 1997.
100. SET Secure Electronic Transaction Specification – Book 2: Programmer's Guide, v1.0, May 1997.
101. SET Secure Electronic Transaction Specification – Book 3: Formal Protocol Definition, v1.0, May 1997.
102. Visa Debit Processing Services (DPS), ATM Terminal Driving System, V-0056001-0510-001, 2013.
103. Payment Card Industry (PCI), Encrypting PIN Pad (EPP), Security Requirements, Version 2.1, January 2009.

Index

U

Underlying sensitive value (USV), 28

V

Vendor documentation, 126–127
Virtualization, 81
Virtual local area network (VLAN), 81

for admin, 90
for application, 88

W

Web application firewalls (WAFs), 81
Web-based transactions, 76–77
White-box cryptography, 139
White papers, 126

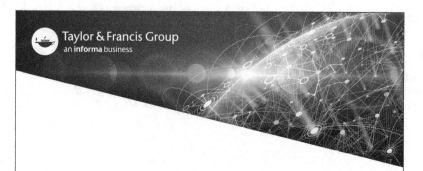